Evangelism for All God's People

EVANGELISM
F O R
ALL GOD'S PEOPLE

LEONARD SANDERSON
A N D
RON JOHNSON

BROADMAN PRESS
NASHVILLE, TENNESSEE

© Copyright 1990 • Broadman Press
All rights reserved
4260-27
ISBN: 0-8054-6027-6
Dewey Decimal Classification: 269.2
Subject Heading: Evangelistic
Library of Congress Catalog Number: 90-32905
Printed in the United States of America

Unless otherwise stated, all Scripture quotations are from the *Revised Standard Version of the Bible,* copyrighted 1946, 1952, © 1971, 1973.

Scripture quotations marked KJV are from the King James Version of the Bible.

Scripture quotations marked GNB are from the *Good News Bible,* the Bible in Today's English Version. Old Testament: Copyright © American Bible Society 1976; New Testament: Copyright © American Bible Society 1966, 1971, 1976. Used by permission.

Library of Congress Cataloging-in-Publication Data

Johnson, Ron, 1949-
     Evangelism for all God's people / Ron Johnson and Leonard
Sanderson.
         p.   cm.
     Includes bibliographical references.
     ISBN 0-8054-6027-6 :
     1. Evangelistic work.   I. Sanderson, Leonard, 1914-
     II. Title.
BV3790.J59   1990
269'.2—dc20   90-32905
                                              CIP

To our colleagues Findley Edge, Reid Hardin, and Dale Cross for their contributions and innovations in marketplace evangelism, and to our wives—Anne Sanderson and Janice Johnson—for their support and interest in this volume.

Contents

Evangelism for All God's People

Introduction: Evangelism for All the People of God

Is it realistic to believe a high-school athlete can talk with his peers about the Lord and the Christian faith as easily and comfortably as he can talk about girls, sports, or an English test?

Can you imagine a college girl in a dorm setting, chatting with her friends without reservation or embarrassment about commitment to Christ?

Can assembly-line workers or labor leaders talk about Jesus and the gospel without being considered fanatical or weird?

A banker in Louisiana seems to talk as effortlessly at coffee break when discussing how his life was turned around during a Lay Witness Mission in his Methodist church as he does when talking about his family, his garden, or a business investment.

A thirty-five-year-old explained his move to a political job: "I believe God may be working especially in the political arena during the next few years. I don't know how you feel when you are called to preach, but I feel a definite call right now to attempt some things in politics which I believe God wants me to be involved in."

A sheriff testified, "I never told anybody during the campaign because I don't think it would have been understood, and I know it would have been misused, but I think it was

God's plan for me to be sheriff." He went on, "I have as much obligation and need to pray for God's direction in this job as if I were pastor of a church."

Do those testimonies sound real? How about the young man in the middle of his seminary career who explained how good he feels about his most recent and toughest decision to date? He said he was sure God was calling him to "full-time Christian service." He had assumed that meant he was to be a preacher.

"After nearly two successful years in seminary, I learned that God might call one to some other occupation. At first it was difficult to admit and painful to explain, but now I feel better about being in seminary than ever before. I believe God wants me to take over the family business and be an active leader in my church and denomination. I especially believe He wants me to be a dedicated evangelistic witness in the business and civic community.

"I would feel comfortable serving a church as interim or mission pastor, or some other church staff position; but I believe my primary mission is in the workaday world.

"Would I have gone to seminary if I had known what I know now? I just might not, but I am inclined to think this is the way God wanted it."

The writers are as sure God called them to be preachers as they are that He called them to salvation. They are completely convinced that He calls some to these special roles of leadership; but they are also confident that most of what the New Testament teaches about "ministry" applies to *all* the people of God regardless of occupation.

Our ultimate goal is that an ever-increasing multitude of Christians will think of themselves as ministers (servants) of Jesus Christ and not just as followers and financial supporters of their church's "hired men."

You see there is no conflict in doing both supportive and ministry roles: Pastors and other vocational religious workers bring their tithes and offerings to support the work of the Lord also. Our special interest in this every-Christian ministry is in the area of evangelism. Our second goal is that pastors, church staffs, and denominational leaders more and more think of themselves as called of God to equip or train all the people of God to be ministers of Christ, especially in evangelism. The book is written, therefore, to be studied by pastors, seminarians, college students, and as many of the people of God as possible.

So, we will be trying to identify the people of God in biblical, historical, and contemporary perspective, including those who are called as coaches, equippers, bishops, or leaders, according to the divinely inspired directions by Paul (see Eph. 4:11*ff*).

Having identified them we will be seeking to present some scriptural and well-tested approaches to doing evangelism in the setting where most Christians find themselves most of the time. Evangelism will be more clearly defined later, but for our present purpose it is "telling the good news about how all people can come to live their lives in touch with God through Christ."

Everyday Evangelism by Everyday People

Most people who read this book will agree that much of their lives they have heard it said all Christians are to be sharers of the good news. Dozens of books have been written on the subject. Titles like *Every Christian's Job*[1], setting forth clearly and biblically that all of God's people are to be engaged in trying to help other people become the people of God, come to mind. Myriads of sermons have been preached on the theme and millions of people have responded with a handshake or signature committing themselves to be "soul-winners" or personal witnesses. Some laypersons, pastors, and denominational people have been faithful to the commitment.

In the 1950s Southern Baptists set aside a Sunday in January to be observed as Evangelism Commitment Day. At first it was to be observed on the first Sunday of the year as a special kind of New Year's resolution. It was later changed to the second Sunday to avoid holiday conflicts. The event has been more or less observed through the years. The following scenario represents what must have happened thousands of times in as many churches.

A Typical Scenario

The pastor believed Jesus' commissions (see Matt. 28:18-20; Mark 16:15; Luke 24:47; John 20:21; Acts 1:8) were for all the people of God, and that evangelism is every Christian's job. He proceeded to be a good pastoral preacher and leader. He spent hours in prayer and study in preparation for the Sunday morning message.

He didn't follow the easy road of catchy quotes to provoke irresponsible approval. He went to God in prayer, to the Bible and other sources for study, and spent hours in thinking through the best possible sermon he could preach to motivate and inspire people to resolve to participate in personal evangelism.

He went from his knees to the pulpit with a sense of divine power. From the time he began preaching he felt the Holy Spirit's leadership. He knew his sermon was interesting, challenging, and forceful. He could see and feel the positive and warm responses of the people. He had never felt better about a sermon. He felt comfortable with a strong invitation for public response.

A strong majority of members present signed pledge cards committing themselves to be personal witnesses in the new year. Not only did the pastor feel good about the message and the response, the people did. The pastor was not only exhausted with excitement, but all the enthusiastic handshakes left his hands stiff and arthritic. He just knew it was to be an unforgettable and celebrated day. As it turned out, it was unforgettable all right—to the pastor's chagrin.

Sure enough, a few faithful souls began some sincere efforts to witness to family, friends and acquaintances. Most of the well-intentioned respondents, however, found that active reality was not as easily executed as spontaneous emotional commitment.

Certainly the pastor was disappointed. Clearly many of the people were frustrated and perturbed. They didn't talk about it as much as the pastor grieved about it. He doubted their sincerity and felt personal failure. Many of them felt guilt.

Some of the people, as they reflected, felt that maybe the pastor came on too strong, maybe he exploited their warm response to his sermon; or maybe he was frustrated by his own failures.

How do you explain the problem? Was the pastor mistaken about the proper application of the Lord's commission? Was the sermon too forceful? Did he come on too strong with the invitation to commitment? Were the people insincere in their response?

In 1922, J. E. Conant gave an answer to a comparable dilemma by saying the pastor and people failed for want of a program.[2] He explained that pastor and people were sincere in their motivation and correct in their commitment, but didn't know how to carry out their resolution. However, some of us have since had excellent program failures to add to the fizzle spectrum.

Some of my programs as pastor, denominational leader, evangelist, and teacher have not had complete success because they were *my* programs. I could use my witnessing approach comfortably, whereas some businessman or auto mechanic might find the same approach awkward at his desk or workbench, however sincere he might be.[3]

A businessman said, "Preacher, you just have to admit that it is more difficult for a layman to go to someone and say, 'I've come out to talk with you about the Lord' and right away reach in his pocket for his New Testament and begin to read from passage to passage."

The pastor explained that what the businessman didn't know was that it isn't all that easy for the pastor, either. Of course if the businessman perceived a problem, there was a problem.

Organizationally and structurally most large Christian denominations and many para-church groups have had excellent evangelism programs. Why is it, then, that most "lay people" sincerely say, "I just have a difficult time talking with people about becoming Christians? I just don't seem to have that gift. I'm not a salesperson type." They are doubtless completely sincere about it. Many have prayed and agonized about it.

Is it possible the programs and presentations, the models and methods, have been conceptualized and communicated from an atmosphere, and written in a language, that feels foreign at the clinic or courthouse, the store or shop, the golf course or garden club, the college campus or supermarket?

Have you ever caught yourself talking "church talk" about religious matters like you talk "baby talk" to small children? In many of our evangelism programs the trainee goes with the trainer: he listens, watches, and memorizes, then tries to reproduce. But often the language doesn't reproduce in the layperson's world.

Without a doubt the method mentioned above is a sound method of training. The Jesus method, no less. But is it sacrilegious to analyze it and examine it? Jesus didn't talk up or down to people. He used the common language of the people more than he used the language of the religious elitist.

Ordinary Language

We have better and better materials and technology, but is it time for another step? How about using more "layperson's" language for "laypersons" to talk to "laypersons"?

Have you noticed how happy people's faces are when they talk about sports or fashions? Have you noticed the animated conversation about politics, cooking, business, or even the weather? Why can't Christians have comfortable conversation at coffee about the Lord, the Christian life, the Bible, or witnessing?

Christian belief and conversion seem to move into some kind of nether world when brought up in conversation. While modern-day Americans feel comfortable approaching most every subject from an analytical or scientific point of view, we all too often tend to approach religious language and discussion as something unnatural, something that cannot be proven or all too abstract to discuss.

But the pattern of the New Testament is that Jesus took religion and moved it into daily life. That's one reason why he took parables as a storytelling motif. He wanted to show that talking about the Father was just as natural as talking about the weather. He wanted to enable people to see God in every aspect of the human experience. Certainly today we need a more comfortable, natural, Jesus-like approach to talking about spiritual matters.

Let's take a cue from the language of the New Testament: "At bottom it is simply straight KOINE of the first century A.D. like that found in the inscriptions of Asia Minor and in the papyri of Egypt." In the papyri of the first century there are "business contracts, bills, deeds, marriage contracts, wills, decrees, love letters . . . anything and everything that made up the life of the people of the time . . . and Koine means the language common to people everywhere . . . It was the means of communication all over the Roman Empire."[4]

Person-centered Witnessing

Our objective is a practical presentation of the good news from the perspective of the home or marketplace rather than exclusively the church building or classroom. While both authors have wide experience "professionally," our actual experiential evangelism emphasis and work have been with persons at home or in the workplace.

This book is church-oriented and church-centered because the church is comprised of the people of God, and all the people of God are to be involved in evangelism. But most of the people to be evangelized (with the exception of children in church homes) are not in church and many are not familiar with church talk.

We are beginning with a basic assumption: the people in your community are not there for the sake of your church. *Your church is there for the sake of the people in the community.* Here we keep in mind the purpose of God in the coming of Jesus into the world. God so loved *people* that He gave Jesus (see John 3:16). He explained His coming: "I am come that they might have life, and that they might have it more abundantly" (John 10:10); ". . . I am not come to call the righteous, but sinners to repentance" (Matt. 9:13); "For the Son of man came not to be ministered unto, but to minister, and to give his life a ransom for many" (Matt. 20:28); ". . . the Son of man is come to seek and to save that which was lost" (Luke 19:10).

When you look at the total ministry of Jesus you immediately are struck by how person-centered it is: the ministry to the woman at the well (see John 4:4-26); healing the nobleman's son (see John 4:46-54); healing the demoniac (see Mark 5:1-17); healing Peter's mother-in-law (see Matt. 8:14-15); and also in feeding the hungry, raising the dead, or the summary statements like he gave John's disciples:

> Go and show John again those things which ye do hear and see: The blind receive their sight, and the lame walk, and the lepers are cleansed, and the deaf hear, and the dead are raised up, and the poor have the gospel preached to them (Matt. 11:4-5, KJV);

or the explanation of the Scripture at Nazareth,

> The Spirit of the Lord is upon me, because he hath anointed me to preach the gospel to the poor; he hath sent me to heal the brokenhearted, to preach deliverance to the captives, and recovering sight to the blind, and to set at liberty them that are bruised, to preach the acceptable year of the Lord (Luke 4:18-19, KJV).

His explanation was, "This day is this Scripture fulfilled in your ears."

Jesus' prayer to the Father was, "I have glorified thee on the earth: I have finished the work which thou gavest me to do" (John 17:4). He glorified the Father by bringing the reality of God to the human experience, by serving people and especially by His death and resurrection to provide salvation for all people. Wasn't this His purpose in founding the church (Matthew 16, 18)?

If your church is there for the benefit of the people, you can understand that the denomination, at every level, is there for the benefit of the churches.

So our approach as authors to pastors, seminarians, church staffs, and all leadership is that we keep in mind the people to be reached as we try to grasp the profound truth that all the people of God are to help all people have an opportunity to become the people of God.

We have written this book together. As such, the reader will note from time to time a synthesis of our ideas. At other times the reader will glean from our personal experiences and individual insights. To aid the reader, we have footnoted our personal experiences, where necessary, so the reader can follow along easily.

Leonard Sanderson
Ron Johnson

1
The Call to Evangelism

Does God call all Christians to evangelism? A college student called for an appointment. When he arrived, and before he was seated, he began: "Brother Sanderson, I know you are wondering why I called you for an appointment. Well, you see, I keep having the feeling God is calling me to evangelism. I talked to my pastor and he told me to talk to you. He said you could probably help me know whether or not God actually calls people to evangelism. What do you think?"

My first thought was that he meets two very important qualifications: He is excited, and he knows how to get to the point. However, his excitement changed to shock when I answered, "Yes, I think God calls all Christians to evangelism."

I then explained what I meant and opened my New Testament to Ephesians 4:11 and assured him that I think God definitely calls and gifts some people to a special ministry of evangelism. I also explained that the passage seems to say that the special calling is particularly to equip all the saints for the ministry of evangelism. Have you asked why it seems so difficult to find particular scriptural passages emphasizing the importance of lay ministries? It is because that is what the Bible is mostly about. The Bible, especially the New Testament, does not make these distinctions between clergy and laymen.

There is no question that God calls people to special ministries, including evangelism and there are occasional special directions and instructions for them (Eph. 4:11; 1 Tim. 3:1-7; 1 Pet. 5:1-4 are examples). However, whatever message you read in the Bible is likely for you. How does God call his people to evangelism? One way is love.

The Love Call

> Of the themes that men have known,
> One supremely stands alone;
> Thro' the ages it has shown,
> 'Tis His wonderful, wonderful love.[5]

The Great Commandment

"Teacher, which is the great commandment in the law?" And he said to him, "You shall love the Lord your God with all your heart, and with all your soul, and with all your mind. This is the great and first commandment. And a second is like it, You shall love your neighbor as yourself. On these two commandments depend all the law and the prophets (Matt. 22:36-40).

John R. W. Stott of London spoke to a world congress on evangelism about the parallelism of the Great Commission (Matt. 28:18-20) and the great commandment (Matt. 22:36-40).[6] I listened to the great man and the great message with deep appreciation and inspiration.[7] As never before I related the great commandment to the Great Commission. Then it occurred to me that they not only belong together, but maybe the great commandment comes first. Maybe, instead of the lines being parallel, they may be perpendicular. Can there be a consistent and sustained obedience to the Great Commission without a commitment to the great commandment to love your neighbor as yourself? Love, worship, and evangelism are inextricably intertwined.

God's love for us, our respondent love for Him, and our love for ourselves (because God attests to our self-worth) inspires our love for others and our desire to minister to their needs.

God's Love for Us

The Lord said to Israel, "I have loved you with an everlasting love; therefore I have continued my faithfulness to you" (Jer. 31:3). Hosea wrote, "When Israel was a child, I loved him" (11:1). Through Malachi, God said to Israel, "I have loved you" (1:2).

The message of God's love for us flows through the New Testament like an artesian well: "God so loved . . . that he gave (Jesus)" (John 3:16); ". . . for the Father himself loves you" (John 16:27); "But God shows his love for us in that while we were yet sinners Christ died for us" (Rom. 5:8); "But God who is rich in mercy, out of the great love with which he loved us, even when we were dead through our trespasses, made us alive together with Christ" (Eph. 2:4-5); "See what love the Father has given us" (1 John 3:1). No wonder one of the first Scripture verses young children begin to quote from memory is "God is love," used repeatedly in the Bible.

Christ's Love for Us

"I live by faith in the Son of God, who loved me and gave himself for me" (Gal. 2:20b); "For the love of Christ controls us" (2 Cor. 5:14); ". . . to know the love of Christ which surpasses knowledge" (Eph. 3:19); "And walk in love, as Christ loved us and gave himself up for us" (Eph. 5:2); "By this we know love, that he laid down his life for us; and we ought to lay down our lives for the brethren" (1 John 3:16).

Our Love for God

Love responds to love. When we see how much God loves us, and how He expresses His love through the Word become flesh, we begin to love Him with a new love. To love Him is to trust His Son to live in us and control our lives (see Rom. 8:9-11; Gal. 2:20).

If Christ lives in us to control our minds and our lives, we begin to think like He thinks and love like He loves. We then are capable of loving our neighbor as ourselves. When we begin to love as Jesus loves we begin to desire new life for others as Christ does.

Since love is "the greatest thing in the world" and it must be because "God is love," how can we know if, or how much, we love God? How can we test our love for anyone? How much do we enjoy His presence? How careful are we to please Him? How can we be sure we are pleasing Him? "Truly, I say to you, as you did it to one of the least of these my brethren, you did it to me" (Matt. 25:40). Look again: "Beloved if God so loved us, we also ought to love one another. No man has ever seen God; if we love one another, God abides in us and his love is perfected in us" (1 John 4:11-12). "We love, because he first loved us" (1 John 4:19).

Our Love for Others

At the Congress on Evangelism just referred to, different denominations held small group discussions. In one of these a prominent pastor, speaking rather defensively, said, "In our denomination the churches do more social work than some who talk about it more, but we do it as a means to an end, and that end is evangelism." At the time I passed it off on the assumption that his cliche was showing, but later when he made the same statement at a major denominational meeting, I decided something else was showing.[8] Why did Jesus feed the hungry, heal the sick, and restore sight to the blind? Matthew wrote that it was compassion (9:36; 14:14; 15:32; 20:24). He used the strongest word for compassion in the Greek language *(splangchna)*. Luke used the same word concerning the raising of the widow's son (7:13). It was Jesus' nature to have compassion for people. He acted out of love in ministering to people's mental and physical needs, just as He did in their spiritual needs.

A businessman friend in Lake Charles, Louisiana, used to say, "Ain't that just like Jesus?" That is not to say that healing the sick or feeding the hungry was as important as saving the lost. It is to say that Jesus had loving compassion for people in all their needs. No doubt the healing of Peter's mother-in-law led to open doors for evangelism. Loving ministries by any church will open evangelism doors.

Philip, who performed the mundane ministry of serving tables (see Acts 6), became one of the outstanding evangelists of the New Testament. He was behaving like Jesus. *Agapé,* the Greek word for love used in most of the preceding passages, will result in all His people behaving like Jesus. Jesus' life of love was filled with all kinds of loving ministries, but His death on the cross was to save us from our sins (see 1 Cor. 15:3). That was His reason for coming into the world (see Matt. 20:28; Luke 5:32; 19:10).

The abundant or superior life He came to provide (see John 10:10) might include other ministries, but the focus is on the full and complete life which begins with a new birth. There is no more conflict between the healing ministry and the saving ministry of Jesus than there is a conflict between ministering medically to a sick child or helping the child become a Christian. Love prompts both. Ministry-based evangelism will be discussed later.

The Quality of Evangelism Motivated by Love

Evangelism may be done for selfish and mundane reasons. People sometimes, thankfully, can come to know the Lord when both our motives and methods are more humanistic than Spirit-led. Mrs. Sunday School Teacher, has your goal of "seeing every member of this class saved before Promotion Day" always been altogether for the glory of God? Well, it was better than no motive.

Mr. Businessman, was your goal "to see all my managers come to know the Lord this year" altogether for their good and the glory of God? Well, praise God for all of them who got saved anyway.

Mr. Shop Foreman, was your goal "to witness to at least one person every day of my life" always purely to please the Lord? Thank God, more people came to know the Lord than if you had no motive. Mr. Pastor, was your goal "to be sure somebody would walk that aisle on Sunday morning" always because you "loved souls so much"? Thank God for those who came to experience the new life anyway.

Mr. Vocational Evangelist, was your desire for a "large number of decisions" always "to honor the precious name of Jesus" or is it just possible there may have been some undisclosed motives? Well, if it were not for selfish motives, some of us would have few motives at all. If it were not for ego, some of us would have very little go at all.

Honestly, we find it painful to criticize what we consider mundane and opportunistic motives in evangelism when millions of God's people seem to have no evangelistic motives at all. Unfortunately, if God could not use less than clean vessels, He would be without vessels. But He deserves better.

The people who need the Lord deserve better. The church deserves better.

> Come, Holy Spirit, heavenly Dove,
> With all Thy quick-'ning pow'rs;
> Come, shed abroad the Saviour's love,
> And that shall kindle ours.[9]

Let's pray for a renewal of love. There are some indications of some such spiritual revival in some places. There are some churches where it is happening and some pastors are out in the forefront giving conscious leadership. There are some workplaces where some "lay people" are quietly being the good news, and that typically leads to opportunities to tell the good news.

I'm thinking of a young businessman, active in his church, president of his company, slightly shy, and very low key, who is being salt and light in his business, civic club, Fellowship of Christian Athletes, Gideons, and with family members.[10] Several have come to know the Lord through his ministry.

Love-motivated evangelism produces its own exciting characteristics. First, there is an exciting intensity about it. For example, Andrew did not make excuses that one cannot witness to relatives. Soon after he had begun to follow Jesus, "He first found his brother Simon, and said to him, 'We have found the Messiah' . . . He brought him to Jesus" (John 1:41-42). Likely the other disciple in the passage was John. If so, he likely found his brother, James, and brought him to Jesus.

After that we read about Peter and Andrew; also James and John. The truth is that witnessing to family members may be difficult if done superficially, ostentatiously, or by mechanical routine. But when love presides, it usually prevails.

In the second place, love-motivated evangelism is effective. A woman in Baton Rouge, Louisiana, because of an injury, was limited in speech and motor control. While attending a neighborhood prayer meeting sponsored by her church, she heard someone mention her ninety-year-old grandfather's name as one who needed salvation. When the meeting was over she asked a friend to drive her to her grandfather's house. When she got there her emotions were so sensitive she could not say what she had planned. Finally, she stammered out, "Grandpa, if you don't trust Jesus soon, you are going to hell." Grandpa got under such conviction, he called another family member and asked for help. The result was that he offered himself for church membership the next Sunday by profession of faith in Jesus.

In the third place, love-motivated evangelism is often done creatively and innovatively. My mother and a neighbor couple were praying for my father's conversion. He boasted that he would never set foot in another church building. Mama and her neighbors knew that Papa Sanderson was stubborn enough that he might risk going on lost forever rather than compromise his foolish boasting. The Presbyterians announced a brush-arbor revival meeting a few miles away. So Mama and our friends the Perrys agreed on a plan: "Aubrey," Mama said, "I know you don't go to church, but you didn't say you wouldn't attend a brush-arbor meeting. You know a lot of your relatives are Presbyterians. Why don't we go to Cloverport, visit your folks and then attend the meeting." A little crafty? Yes, but my guess is that Papa was glad to have a chance to save face, anyway.

I wish I had learned the preacher's name. I listened to my father tell the story many times; "That preacher knew how to get to me. I think God must have been in it. He talked about parents and their influence on their children. I knew I didn't want my son to follow in my footsteps." God's Spirit seemed to be leading in numerous events the next day. Before the day was over Papa received the Lord in his life. Love finds a way. My own conversion years later was another step in that same familial love.

The call to evangelism includes an understanding of God's love for us and our love for others. It includes an understanding of what happens when people "convert." But is there a basic element that is just as important in the salvation story as the love of God for us and our love of God expressed toward others? What about need? Plain, ordinary need. How does it affect us? Does God need for us to be saved?

God's Need

It may seem strange to discuss God as needing anything. After all, wouldn't it seem reasonable that the God of the universe has everything He needs? It depends on how we choose to define the word, need. For frail human beings, *need* describes what we believe we have to have to exist. But *need* as it relates to God takes on an entirely new dimension.

A. T. Robertson once wrote, "The infinite God cannot be grasped by the human mind either by inquiry or by revelation."[11] An ancient Chinese proverb says that once you define God, He is finished as God. Certainly, God is larger than our definitions. The saying is true. . . . "God defined is God finished."

If this is true it would appear that God needs to help us know who He is. After all, Moses posed this question directly to God. "If I come to the people of Israel and say to them, 'The God of your fathers has sent me to you,' and they ask me, 'What is his name?' what shall I say to them?" (Ex. 3:13). God told the people He was the eternal God.

Throughout the Old Testament God sought to make Himself known to the people. Time and time again God describes Himself to the people. In Exodus, God said to Moses, ". . . I will take you for my people, and I will be your God . . ." (6:7). He showed His fatherly protection of the nation as He brought them out of the land of the Egyptians, as He defeated nation after nation in the Books of Joshua and Judges.

In Jeremiah 31:9 God says, ". . . for I am a father to Israel . . ." Likewise, in Hosea 11:1, Israel is called "my son" by God. The parallel of God's love for Israel and Hosea's love for Gomer, his wife, is apparent in Hosea. In the Psalms the image of God as Father is clear. Psalm 68:5 pictures God as, "Father of the fatherless and protector of widows . . ." God is seen in Psalm 103:13 as pitying His children.

Various attributes were given by God to the writers of the Old Testament to reveal Himself. He is called the eternal God, the most high God, the God of hosts, the mighty God, the Lord God of the Fathers, a God of jealous love. It is evident that God's need is to reveal Himself to us so that we may know Him.

The New Testament documents God's need to make Himself known to us in the record of His Son Jesus. Jesus was the fulfillment of God's supreme revelation of Himself to mankind. Jesus said, "And he who sees me sees him who sent me" (John 12:45).

In the Old Testament and in the New Testament God needed to draw all persons to Himself. The picture of God in Genesis is one of fellowship with mankind in the cool of the Garden. Sin destroyed that relationship. God, however, thwarted our sinfulness by Christ's sacrifice on the cross thereby reconciling us to himself. Jesus said, ". . . and I, when I am lifted up from the earth, will draw all men to myself" (John 12:32). God needs to draw us to Himself. That is his nature as the God who saves.

The Bible promises that when Jesus returns He will receive us unto Himself; that where He is there we may be also (John 14:3). Certainly, one could not doubt that the God who walked in fellowship with mankind in the cool of the Garden longs to do so again when He comes to receive His own.

Certainly then the answer to the question above, "Does God need for us to be saved?" is an overwhelming, "Yes." God needs for us to recognize our lostness and come to Him for salvation. God is not content to let us condemn ourselves. That's why He made a way for us to be saved. He is not willing for anyone to perish. God cannot overlook our sins and the terrible consequences they bring. That's the whole reason for the revelation of Himself in the Old Testament and the sending of His Son in the New Testament. John 3:16 takes on an even fuller meaning when we understand the yearning in the heart of God, the need of God, to love us so much that not one should perish.

Luke 15 is a prime example of God's need to restore us to Him. The lost sheep causes the shepherd to focus his attention on the one who wandered. He is not content until the lost is found. When the woman finds the lost coin, there is rejoicing. She seeks diligently for it. She sweeps and cleans her house searching for that which is lost. The father cannot rest until his son is returned. We sense from the Scripture that he must have watched day after day for his son's return. When the son came home there was intense joy and celebration. Luke 15:10 assures us that there is just as much rejoicing in heaven when a lost person comes home to God. God has a need to reclaim what He has set aside for Himself.

Our Need

If God has a need to reveal His love to us, then what need do we, His creation, have? Do we not have a need to know God? Mankind has searched for meaning in life for centuries. Thousands of books have been published that have sought to define ultimate human need and satisfy it. Some have said man's need can be fulfilled through self-understanding. Others say human need can be fulfilled through meditation or therapy.

But Christians through the ages have testified that no manmade cure ever satisfied their need like Jesus. God created human beings with a need for Him. That void can never be fulfilled by anything else. Certainly the verses of the song ring true . . . "No one ever cared for me like Jesus."

Multitudes of Christians have had lives turned around when they met Jesus. Every need expressed in their lives has been fulfilled after meeting the Master. Not long ago, I visited a seventy-four-year-old man who had been an alcoholic all his life.[12] He was withered and drawn from years of drink. His mind was filled with all kinds of scary images. He saw things on the wall and on the ceiling that seemed to be coming to get him. He described snakes that crawled out of the lake behind his house and into his room to strike him.

Family members grieved that he was being tormented so. They called for me to come and visit him. Surely God had paved the way because on the day I visited him, his mind was clear. He and I talked for some time and he described his torment in vivid detail. I asked him if he had ever come to the place where he had received Jesus as his personal Savior. He said he had not.

I shared the simple Gospel message with him, showing him Scriptures that would lead him to faith in Christ. After about an hour, he bowed his head and received Jesus as his personal Savior. Until his death, a year later, he slept with his Bible by his bedside. He read it daily. Never again did he have the awful dreams he had once had. His images of things coming to get him disappeared. His language changed. His smile was evident. Family members said he never smoked again, nor drank another drop of alcohol. He died quietly in his sleep. Christ transformed his life. His emotions and his physical life improved after he found Jesus.

Recently, I talked to another man who owned a company in a nearby city.[13] He had been dramatically saved just three years earlier. He had all the material possessions that one could desire. But he lacked inner peace. He hungered for something else. His own testimony indicated that it was only when he was saved that he found the fulfillment of his need. He needed Christ. He needed to fill the void that was apparent in his life. His life is testimony to the fact that a life devoid of Christ is incomplete.

She was a poor lady. I dropped in to visit her because she had been sick and was a lovely Christian lady who had supported the church where I served as interim pastor for all her life.[14] Now, in failing health she was unable to come to the church she loved or even talk much about the Lord she served. With gasping voice she managed to talk to me about Jesus.

She told me how Jesus had carried her through the hard times and how she had been blessed by Him. It was obvious to me, looking at her humble home, that she had never been a person of many possessions. But deep in her aging eyes was a sparkle put there by her relationship with Christ. The void in her life had long ago been filled by the Savior.

Whether in riches or in poverty, the need for Christ exists in all of us. Like a powerful magnet, God reaches toward us out of His need to love and save us. Like elements of iron attracted by the magnet our lives reach up to Him through faith in Christ to meet the need for salvation and love that only God can give. How beautiful it is when God reaches down for us and we reach out for Him.

The Gospel in Today's World

Unfortunately, many individuals all over the world could testify that not a person has ever told them about Jesus, though millions of them have known Christians all their lives. If people are to come face to face with their need for Christ and if God's need to rescue men from the damnation of sin is ever to be accomplished, surely Christians must take seriously the call to obedience that the Great Commission commands.

Lyle Schaller in his book, *It's A Different World,* says it's harder to minister in today's world than ever before.[15] He is certainly right. There are dozens of factors that mitigate against the church's witness. But the challenge to evangelize has never been more real than today.

The lostness of our world is staggering. James Surgener, in his book, *Lost,* says that literally billions are lost in our world.[16] According to the Southern Baptist Home Mission Board we in the United States are living in a nation of ever-increasing lostness. Some 170 million people are lost in the United States. (SBC Home Mission Board Research Dept.)

In the face of such lostness, however, The Princeton Religion Research Center in its report, *The Unchurched American . . . 10 years later,* found, ". . . that the churches have not made any inroads into attracting the unchurched over the past decade . . ."[17] Yet, the same report indicates that 72 percent of people believe that Jesus is God or the Son of God, up from 64 percent a decade ago. Why this paradox? How can churches fail to grow when people increasingly claim to believe in the deity of Christ?

Certainly two factors impact this paradox. One is the ever-increasing threat of universalism into our theology. Universalism is the doctrine or the belief that God through his grace revealed in Christ will ultimately save every member of the human race from sin, eternal punishment, damnation, and hell regardless of how unrighteous they might have been here on earth. When was the last time you heard an old-fashioned sermon or Sunday School lesson on hell? Dr. Roy Fish, professor of evangelism at Southwestern Baptist Theological Seminary, tells of a meeting he attended where four well-known evangelicals were presenting papers on the destiny of the lost. Dr. Fish said that in their presentations, "The word hell was not used one time in that conference. Not one mention of final judgment which consigned unrepentant men to eternal darkness."[18] We do not like to preach about hell hell today. We had rather preach about the love of God all the time. Certainly God is love. But God is also a judge of the righteous and the wicked. Do most church members believe this?

To believe that everyone is going to get to heaven one day by and by is to sap the energy of evangelism. Christ never taught or preached such a gospel. He spent more time than anyone else warning of a hell to flee.

Every Christian must realize that the passion of the early church was evangelism. It was to tell others about Christ. That need has not changed today. We must warn our loved ones, neighbors, friends, business acquaintances, and strangers that a choice must be made. We must, in the words of Joshua of old, choose whom we will serve. There *is* a heaven to gain and a hell to shun. The people of God must capture a vision of millions and millions who are lost and bound for hell. We cannot hope they will get to heaven. We cannot assume their own goodness will get them there. Rather we must confront them with the claims of Christ and allow them to make the choice to receive Him as personal Savior.

A second factor necessary to confronting people with the message of Christ is helping them to understand the demands of the gospel. The gospel of Christ is radical. It calls for an entire reorientation to life. It calls for being "sold out" to Christ; dead to self.

Unfortunately, most sermons and personal testimonies today are composed of "feel good" theology or a "gospel of success." We cannot help but reflect on Christ's lifestyle who taught us that success could be defined by the life given to holiness, not things. Somehow, it is hard to understand a gospel of prosperity against the backdrop of world hunger and devastation. It is hard to justify a "feel good," noninvolved theology and consider the life of a Mother Teresa who ministers in the poverty and sickness of the slums of Calcutta, India. If the gospel is to be understood in today's world, we who are Christians must learn how to contextualize it through ministry to others.

It is time to take advantage of the openness of searching people who claim to have had a religious experience at some time in their lives. In short, it is time to reclaim our evangelistic roots. Evangelicals are a people committed to sharing Jesus. Our world demands we do so today.

Just recently, I spoke to a man who was gripped with conviction.[19] He told me how he had been a Christian for forty years and never once had witnessed. He had a burden for a friend of his who he believed was lost. "I have got to know if he is saved or not." he explained. This man's sense of concern for his friend's salvation had moved him to the point of action. This kind of concern and urgency must be felt by all Christians if we are going to be true to the commission from Christ.

The Great Commission

Shortly after the close of World War II, Martin Niemöller spoke in the chapel service of The Southern Baptist Theological Seminary.[20] The eminent German pastor told of a dream he had after the death of Adolf Hitler. In his dream he saw Hitler before the Lord on Judgment Day. When the infamous dictator was asked why he had never surrendered his life to Jesus he answered that he had never been told about Jesus. Niemöller, in his dream as in awakened memory, recalled that he had had an opportunity to witness to Hitler and did not take advantage of it. How many of us could identify?

You can be sure that no person acquainted with the New Testament could ever say, "I didn't know I am supposed to tell others about Jesus." The writing evangelists were faithful to report Jesus' commission.

From Behind Closed Doors

The most forceful was John's record of what Jesus said on the first Lord's Day. You recall that Jesus appeared to the disciples, without Thomas, on that evening as they met behind closed doors for fear of the Jews. When he had allayed their fears by saying, "Peace be unto you, he went on to say, "as my Father hath sent me, even so send I you." This had to be one of the most extraordinary moments of all their exciting experiences with Jesus. They had heard that he was alive. Now, here He was! Dare they blink their eyes for fear He won't be there? Most of them were seeing Him for the first time since His death. Certainly they had a clearer concept of His ministry now than ever before.

Some of His former words took on new meaning then. They understood better than ever why He came to the world in the person of Jesus of Nazareth. Naturally everything He said now in this exciting setting had even more significance. It was as if He were saying, "Now that you have a new understanding of why I came into the world, now that you have witnessed my death and resurrection, I want to tell you that if it was important that I came into the world on this reconciling mission it is just as important that you tell other people about it."

From the Mount of Olives

How about the call from the mount of Olives? When they came together they evidently expected something significant to occur. So they asked if this would be the time of restoring the kingdom to Israel. Indeed, they did not yet fully grasp the meaning of His mission, did they? His answer was that there were some things beyond the scope of their present understanding, but not to worry about it. There were some things exceedingly important and highly relevant at the present moment: "But you shall receive power when the Holy Spirit has come upon you; and you shall be my witnesses in Jerusalem and in all Judaea and Samaria and to the end of the earth" (Acts 1:8).

How do you describe what happened next? We have to settle for what Luke, by divine inspiration, reported in Acts 1: While they looked on, gravity lost its grip on Jesus, His feet began to leave the surface of ground, He began to rise about the tops of the olive trees, and higher and higher until

a cloud received him out of their sight. And while they looked steadfastly toward heaven as he went up, behold, two men stood by them in white apparel; which also said, Ye men of Galilee, why stand ye gazing up into heaven? This same Jesus, which is taken up from you into heaven, shall so come in like manner as ye have seen him go into heaven" (vv. 9b-11, KJV).

We would not dare use that passage to prove where heaven is, but taking the beloved physician's word for it would cause us to believe those friends of Jesus never forgot the Master's last words before that spectacular departure.

From the Mountain in Galilee

The call to evangelism most often quoted was the report by Matthew. This political office holder who had received a personal call from Christ, and had immediately responded with a notable marketplace evangelism demonstration (Luke 5:29), gave this most familiar evangelistic call from our Lord. The story begins with the sixteenth verse of Matthew 28.

The eleven disciples kept their appointment to meet Jesus on the mountain in Galilee. When was the appointment made? We know that following the supper with His disciples, He told them about some of the events to follow and said, after His being raised "I will go before you into Galilee" (Matthew 26:32, KJV). After He was raised He told the women to tell the disciples to go to Galilee where they would see him (see Matthew 28:10). We do not know the details about how they knew when to meet Him, or how they knew which was "the" mountain.

Was there some particular mountain spot to which they retreated which they would all recognize as "the" mountain? We know for certain what happened when they got there: When they saw him they "worshipped him."

Worship and Evangelism

Can there be evangelism without worship? We know full well one student can tell another student about Jesus over a soft drink between classes without any kind of "worship service." The same can occur between workers at the assembly line or office. There will be no consistent and sustained personal evangelism without the regular practice of worship.

Can there be worship without evangelism? This question may blow our minds about definitions of worship and evangelism. We know there can be worship "services" without evangelism. We know that people who regularly attend worship services worship more, and more effectively. But candor demands we all admit many hours spent in the worship place without worship, and it is not all the fault of the worship leaders. Most of us who have served as worship leaders must also admit there have been times when our deliberate planning has not given worship top priority.

We are also aware there can be times of authentic worship in private. But ask yourself this question: Can there be genuine worship privately or publicly, on a sustained basis, without a desire to share that experience with friends, family members, neighbors, and even unknown people?

When worship becomes more substantive in the gathered church, evangelism will be more evident in the scattered church in the marketplace. Jesus gave the call to evangelism in an atmosphere of worship. How about the private meeting with the disciples on the evening of resurrection day? How about the Mount of Olives at the day of the ascension? Were those worshipful moments?

Of course everybody did not immediately worship on the mountain that day. "Some doubted." The doubters cannot be easily identified. We do not know who all was there. We know the eleven were there. We know there was at least one occasion when Jesus appeared to over 500 people (see 1 Cor. 15:6). Some think this was the time. That would help clear the eleven. But, is it all that important to clear them? Can doubt, like fear, be a wholesome and valuable experience? Have the most faithful and devoted followers of Christ sometimes been doubters? People who "think" they have never doubted might well ascertain whether or not they have ever "thought." Another helpful attribute is honesty. The more mature we become, the less we are bothered by occasional doubts. Following the worship and doubt on their appointment with Jesus, He spoke to them of His authority.

Authority

So Jesus talked with the people who were present about His *authority* to call them (and us) to evangelism. "All authority (not *power* as in the Greek word *dunamis,* from which we get our word dynamite) has been given to me in heaven and on earth." He was saying He has the right to give the evangelism call.

The disciples and some others had come to appreciate His authority and power on earth. Now He was reminding them that He was going back to the Father as He was before the incarnation, and so He had authority in heaven also. He had talked with the Father about this in the great intercessory prayer (see John 17).

Assignment

After establishing His authority, He gave them and all Christians an *assignment,* "Going therefore disciple all nations . . ." It is not "teach" all nations. There is another word for teach which He used later. He was saying "disciple" or *"make disciples."* Obviously they (and we) have no power to change people's lives in making disciples. That work belongs to Christ (see 2 Cor. 5:17).

He was commanding His disciples to "make disciples" in the sense that Philip made disciples in Samaria (see Acts 8:4-8,12); in the sense that Peter made disciples in Caesarea (see Acts 10:44-48); and the sense in which Barnabas found the scattered believers making disciples in Antioch (see Acts 11:19-26).

The command is to announce the good news and tell people how to become disciples by the power of the Spirit. There are no geographical, political, or racial limits to the command: "disciple all the nations." The word, usually translated *nations,* here is the Greek word, *ethnos,* from which we get our word *ethnic.* Sometimes it is translated *race, heathen, Gentiles.* It is clear that the Lord's command, like the gospel itself, is to be effective for all kinds of people, and is to be given to peoples everywhere.

The call to evangelize does not end with the initial announcement of the good news, or the "beginning of salvation." Gaines S. Dobbins used to tell the story of the theological student who asked his teacher, "Is conversion the end of salvation?" The professor answered, "Yes, the front end."

Jesus made baptism a part of the "Great Commission." You see the command has not been obeyed until the believer has been publicly initiated. Baptism was the New Testament "public profession." It was not "walking the aisle," or "praying the prayer." The aisle is usually the nearest route from the church pew to where the receiver is standing in the church building. The "prayer" usually includes repentance and an expression of faith in the Lord. Circumstances may necessitate some delay in baptism for the new believer; but there is no question about the New Testament order, method, or urgency of this pictorial demonstration of death, burial, and resurrection. The "soul winner" has not "won a soul" by merely getting a handshake, or a quotation from a prospect. This decision involves a life commitment and the new life follows a prescribed process.

The command is not concluded with baptism. Now Jesus used the customary work for *teach:* "teaching them to observe all that I commanded you." Notice that it is not merely baptizing them and teaching them, but teaching them to *observe all that I commanded you*. Here he touched on the lordship of life. They could not be disciples until they learned what the disciple life was. While the disciple life instruction lasts a lifetime, it is to begin immediately. We will discuss the beginning of the new life more later, but suffice it here to say the call to evangelism is a call to help people enter a new life process in which they continue to need instruction as long as they live.

Assurance

The call includes *assurance* of the presence of the Lord Himself "all the days." All the people of God are called to evangelize and all the people of God have the assurance of the presence of the Lord with them in the process. We are strongly tempted to recoil from the commission on the grounds that we are not gifted or are not the salesperson type. We may be correct. Thankfully, that is not a prerequisite. He never mentions that, even remotely. He simply promises His presence to those who obey His command.

What does He command us to be and do? What do we do to people when we evangelize them? We give them the *gospel, the good news.*

Good News

"Have you heard the good news? A wonderful thing has happened." If someone calls you on the telephone or bursts into your room or office with those words you usually give immediate and cheerful attention. Everyone welcomes good news. That is the way the early church burst upon the world of the first and second centuries. It was not mere good news. It was extraordinary good news. That is what the word evan-

gelism is all about. To some people in the first century it was
the joyful announcement of the long awaited messiah coming
to rescue the world from tyrannical rule. To all who understood it, it was the good news that Jesus had come to give
new, complete, and meaningful life to all who would trust
themselves to Him.

God had created mankind the way he was supposed to be:
in the image and after the likeness of God, and capable of a
high and holy relationship with God. Of course that kind of
being was not a robot, incapable of thinking and making
decisions. The beings which God created made the wrong
choice and forfeited their relationship with God. Jesus was
God coming to the world in the person of a human being to
make it possible for that relationship to be restored and for
God's creation to become what he was supposed to be in the
first place. That was good news.

Try to recall the best news you ever heard and relive the
excitement of the occasion. In that mood you can better understand the excitement of what happened one day in a synagogue in Nazareth. Jesus had returned to Galilee for what is
usually referred to as the "Early Galilean Ministry." Luke described Jesus' Galilean ministry succinctly as having three
characteristics: (1) In the power of the Spirit, (2) growing
fame, and (3) using the synagogues, not only as a place of
habitual worship, but a marketplace for evangelism (see
Luke 4:14).

Now in his home town of Nazareth, for the first time in a
while, His visit to the synagogue on the sabbath day would
create excitement among the regular worshippers. Their increasingly famous son had returned. He stood up to read, either voluntarily or by request. Someone gave Him the book
of the prophet Isaiah. He opened the book and found the
place (Can you just see Him unrolling the scroll on the one

end and rerolling the other end as He found the place?) where it was written,

> The Spirit of the Lord is upon me, because he has anointed me to preach the good news to the poor. He has sent me to proclaim release to the captives and the recovering of sight to the blind, to set at liberty those who are oppressed, to proclaim the acceptable year of the Lord (Luke 4:18-19).

Then the suspense began: "And he closed the book, and gave it back to the attendant, and sat down; and the eyes of all in the synagogue were fixed on him" (v. 20). Now look at the timing: then He said, "Today this scripture has been fulfilled in your hearing." The Isaiah passage which he read (61:1*f*) was highly significant. Isaiah was picturing the Jubilee year and the release of the captives and return from the Babylonian exile with the hope of the Messiah prominent in their minds. The scripture Jesus read and the following several chapters in Isaiah were extremely significant to the Hebrew people. For Him to suggest that those promises were now being fulfilled was packed with emotion. To say it was good news would be the understatement of the year.

When He died the shameful death on the cross, His most loyal followers must have thought they misunderstood Jesus' promise. After the resurrection hope was renewed. So they began to announce the good news with tireless zeal and excitement. In their day and culture it was like a town crier going from group to group announcing the marvelous good news of victory. In our day it would be like the top news anchors of television being called in from their homes or vacations to face the microphones. So the early Christians exhausted their vocabularies of words and forms of words meaning good news.

The English verb "to evangelize" is merely a transliteration of the Greek verb *euaggelizo*. It means *to bring glad tidings, to announce or publish a message, to announce the gospel, declare glad tidings*. It is used fifty-five times in the New Testament. The English noun form is "evangel" (*euaggelion* in the Greek). It is used seventy-seven times in the New Testament and is usually translated "gospel." In the New Testament Luke used the verb and Mark used the noun, both to bring a similar message concerning the spread of the gospel. Paul used the noun "gospel" a great deal. You can spread it (2 Cor. 11:7), teach it (Eph. 6:19), announce it (1 Cor. 9:14), chatter it (1 Thess. 2:2), make it known (2 Cor. 11:7), or accept it (2 Cor. 11:4).[21]

Another similar word in the New Testament is the English word "evangelist" from the Greek *euaggelistes*. It refers to a messenger of good tidings. Herschel Hobbs points out related English words with which we are familiar: preach, teach, disciple, and write.[22] In all these cases the idea is good news. So what do you do for people when you evangelize them? You tell them the good news. It is basically good news about Jesus. Gaines Dobbins wrote: "The good news was Jesus himself—who he was, what he said, what he did, and how he changed the lives of those whom he touched."[23] Dobbins also pointed out the appropriateness of the journalistic formula for reporting: the five w's—the who, what, where, when, why, and sometimes how.[24] Certainly this is a good formula for telling the good news.

What Is the Good News?

Let's let John, the divinely inspired writer, tell us: "In him was life, and the life was the light of men. The light shines in the darkness, and the darkness has not overcome it" (John 1:4-5); "And the Word became flesh and dwelt among us"

(1:14); "No one has ever seen God; the only Son, who is in the bosom of the Father, he has made him known" (1:18); "He came to his own home, and his own people received him not. But to all who received him, who believed in his name, he gave power to become children of God" (1:11-12). He is "the Lamb of God, who takes away the sin of the world" (1:29); "We have found the Messiah" (1:41); "We have found him of whom Moses and also the prophets wrote" (1:45); "For God so loved the world that he gave his only Son, that whoever believes in him should not perish but have eternal life" (3:16); Contrasted with the thief who "comes only to steal and kill and destroy; I came that they might have life, and have it abundantly" (10:10);

> Christ Jesus, who, though he was in the form of God, did not count equality with God a thing to be grasped, but emptied himself, taking the form of a servant, being born in the likeness of men. And being found in human form he humbled himself and became obedient unto death, even death on a cross (Phil. 2:5-8).

Marvelous, indefinable, unfathomable, good news!

What do we do when we evangelize? We give to the people the good news. In the marketplace, as well as in the Bible study group, we spread the good news; we live it, we teach it, we announce it, we chatter it, we gossip it. We seek to live: without ostentation, hypocrisy, bigotry, selfishness, piousity, pride, and greed. We seek to supply love, joy, peace, patience, kindness, goodness, faithfulness, gentleness, and self-control. Through Christ-like living (vocationally and avocationally), and with our language (spoken and body) we will seek to "bear witness" (maturion), another New Testament word, to Jesus Christ.

Bad News

We often complain that news people in the media give us only the bad news. We would be even more dishonest if we give only the good news. Of course the word *gospel* means good news. As we have said, evangelism is telling the good news. The English word *gospel* is from the old English *god-spell: god; good* plus *spel:* news. Nevertheless, good news is good news because there is bad news. "It is on the backdrop of the blackness of sin that the brightness of salvation to righteousness is accentuated."[25] There is a lot of bad news in the world, and always has been.

War is bad news . . . so is oppression, political corruption, bribery, all the evil practices of social structures and institutions. But bad news is more personal than that. It is anything that displeases God. All the "works of the flesh" (Gal. 5:19) are bad news for the world. But not only those sins of commission, because irresponsibility and failure to do what we ought to do is sinful, bad news (see Jas. 4:17).

In order for people to understand their need for the good news they must understand the bad news. All people have sin in their lives. The reality of sin is so clear to Bible writers that they don't argue the subject. Evidence is found on nearly every page. Paul left little to the imagination in Romans 1:18—3:20. In Romans 3:23 and 5:12 he emphasized the universality of sin. "All have sinned." "Therefore as sin came into the world through one man and death through sin, and so death spread to all men because all have sinned."

The Bad News Is Personal

Sin and evil are not only bad because they are universal, but because they are personal. The people closest to Jesus recognized the possibility of their personal guilt, even in His betrayal, "Is it I, Lord?" (Matt. 26:22). It could not be more personal or explicit than John made it: "If we say we have no sin, we [note the first person, plural] we deceive ourselves, and the truth is not in us. If we say we have not sinned, we make him a liar and his word is not in us" (1 John 1:8,10).

Many Greek words for sin are used in the New Testament. Translated they come out: *misdeed, injustice, sin, disbelief, unfaithfulness, unbelief, ungodliness, enmity, wickedness,* and *transgression.*

Dr. Frank Stagg wrote:

> The total man is in trouble beyond his power to remedy. He is in trouble in his thinking, in his emotional responses, in his volitional choices, in his moral values, in his bodily expressions, in his relationship to God, to other people and to things.[26]

Sin is bad news because it separates people from God (Gen. 2:17; Ezek. 18:4; Rom. 6:23).

Good News Is Personal

Bad news is personal and good news is personal. There is a sense in which all evangelism is personal. Each individual must hear and receive the gospel for herself or himself. Another sense in which it is personal is that all people of God are to tell the good news. As persons hear and believe the good news, and their lives are changed, the structures of society will begin to be changed.

This is necessary because some of the bad news is structural and social in its expression. Delos Miles offers an excellent definition of evangelism: "Evangelism is being, doing, and telling the gospel of the kingdom of God, in order that by the power of the Holy Spirit persons and structures may be converted to the lordship of Jesus Christ."[27]

We have discussed what we do to people when we evangelize them. Now let's look at this question: What happens to people when they are evangelized? Suppose you have a friend who works at the next desk at the office. In your conversations with her, and in her daily life-style you have decided she needs new life in the Lord. Your love of God and for her has motivated you to witness to her. Besides you also believe the Lord has commanded you to witness to her. You feel confident that you know what the good news is. So now that you are going to witness to her as the Holy Spirit leads, what do you expect to see happen in her life?

Conversion

The wide variety of words and phrases used to describe the experience creates some problem when discussing what occurs when persons become sons and daughters of God. We talk about "becoming a Christian," "being saved," "trusting Jesus," "getting converted," "receiving Christ," or "accepting Jesus." In reporting evangelistic results we use phrases like "prayed the prayer," "walked the aisle," "went forward," "made a profession of faith," or "joined the church."

This medley may account for some of the stumbling for words as we try to talk with people about the Lord. The New Testament used words like: "believed," "gave heed," "received his word," "those who were being saved," "believers were added to the Lord," "disciples multiplied," and "believers were added." We are using the word "conversion," and it has its limitations.

What Conversion Means

The basic idea in the New Testament words for conversion *(epistrephein* and *strephein)* is to *turn, return,* or *change directions*. The same idea is conveyed sometimes by another word (Greek *metaneoin*) usually translated *repent*. (We normally think of repentance as a part of the conversion experience. It will be discussed later.) Conversion, then, is turning from something to something. It is turning from sin and self to Christ and God, it is the changing of one's mind and life in the direction of God. The subject is easy to oversimplify, also to overcomplicate.

Sam Jones, a unique American Methodist evangelist of another generation, told the story of a bishop delivering a profound theological discourse on conversion. (It could have been repentance. He could have also been Baptist.) In the middle of his long and meticulous sermon as the audience got sleepier and sleepier, an old man on the front seat jumped up and said, "Brother Bishop, I would like to say a word . . ." The bishop, surprised, and somewhat exasperated, said, "Alright, Brother Jones. I'm sure anything you would say would be helpful. What would you like to say?" The old man began running down the church aisle toward the back door, screaming, "I'm going to hell! I'm going to hell! I'm going to hell!" When he got to the end of the aisle he returned down the aisle, yelling, "Now I'm going to heaven. I'm going to heaven. I'm going to heaven." He then looked up at the bishop and said, "Brother Bishop, that's what conversion is; I was on my way to hell. Then I came to see myself and my sin. I turned around and began to follow Jesus. Now I'm on my way to heaven." Well, he was probably oversimplifying it, just as the bishop was overcomplicating it, but he was going in the right direction.

The New Testament speaks often of people turning to the Lord. "And all the residents of Lydda and Sharon saw him, and they turned to the Lord" (Acts 9:35). In Lystra when Paul was preaching to the Greeks "that you should turn from these vain things to a living God" (Acts 14:15). Paul was sent to the

Gentiles "that they may *turn from darkness* to light and from
the power of Satan to God" (Acts 26:18). This meant turning
from ignorance to knowledge, from evil to good, from slavery
to freedom, from retreat to victory. Is every Christian not
called to do the same thing Paul was called to do?

Why Conversion Is Necessary

Evangelism is necessary because conversion is necessary.
Conversion is necessary because mankind is far from God
and going in the wrong direction. Sin is not a popular subject.
Some of us can remember when we thought the only thing
preachers preached about was sin. We also knew in advance
which sins would receive priority attention. There may be
some of this kind of preaching now, but a more serious tendency is just to pass sin by as being too negative to preach
and teach about at all.

Foy Valentine, speaking before a state-wide Southern
Baptist evangelism conference in Louisiana, listed one of the
weaknesses of present-day preaching and teaching—the silence about sin. Several years ago the noted psychiatrist Karl
Menninger wrote a book entitled, *Whatever Became of Sin?*
He pointed out the psychological need for people to recognize
and confess their sins.

Of course most people are rather articulate in confessing
other people's sins. A pastor friend said that one Sunday he
gave the invitation and a young man came down the aisle.
Thinking he was coming to accept Jesus as his Savior, he
extended his hand to receive the man. The man spoke clearly
to the pastor and said, "I am coming to confess my wife's sins
and to rededicate her life to Christ." Wives' sins are easily
discernable to husbands. It is easy for the rich to talk about
the sins of the poor, and easy for the poor to speak fluently of
the sins of the rich. It is simple to recognize the sins of the

other race, or country, or political party. The sins of the
young are so clear to the old. Of course preachers are professional confessors of other people's sins.

The closer we are to God the easier it is to detect our own
sins. The more we read the Bible the more aware we are of
the need for conversion. Dr. Stagg wrote

> that the salvation required must be more than information
> for the mind, the advantage of a good example, external ap-
> plications of a religious rite, a tranquilizer for the emotions,
> or ascetic discipline to curb bodily impulses. The salvation
> must come from a source higher than man, and it must in-
> clude the cleansing and renewal of the total person.[28]

Mankind needs changing. That changing of the mind and
life is called conversion. God and persons cooperate in leading individuals to the conversion experience. The early
church was thoroughly sensitive to the necessity of this
divine-human collaboration. When Paul and Barnabas reported on their evangelistic work to the church at Antioch it
was "all that God had done *with* them" (Acts 14:27, author's
italics). The same words were used in reporting to the Jerusalem Conference (Acts 15:4). The word *with* (Greek *meta*)
means participation as well as nearness. God was their part-
ner in leading people to conversion.[29]

God and Conversion

"As in creation, so also in redemption, the fundamental
truth is expressed in the language of Genesis 1:1, 'In the beginning God.'"[30] While conversion involves a person's turning to God, it must not be forgotten that the decision to turn
to God, or return to God, is a response to God's provision,
power, and prompting.

Mankind can give himself to God only because God has

given Himself to mankind. God takes the initiative in conversion. People do not discover God, even with the help of the evangelist. God is self-revealed to people. Luke, who tells us more directly about evangelism than anybody else in the early church, makes it clear that man cannot provide the two main factors in evangelism, the Spirit of God and the Word of God.[31]

The "son of man came to seek and to save the lost" (Luke 19:10). In Luke 15 the shepherd seeks the sheep, the woman seeks the coin, and the father seeks both sons. We love because He first loved us (1 John 4:19). Jesus said, "this is why I told you that no one can come to me unless it is granted to him by the Father" (John 6:65). "You did not choose me, but I chose you" (John 15:16). All this is true with those who turn from sin to salvation in the initial conversion experience, those Christians who return to the Lord after they have wandered away, and those who witness to others.

Oversimplification of this profound doctrine results in two opposing errors: (1) The most frequent error in modern evangelism, that of making all our evangelism plans and then simply asking God, in a closing prayer, to bless these plans we have made; and (2) the excuse that we not run ahead of God, the argument that we must not witness "until the Spirit leads."

J. I. Packer reminds us of two familiar stories: first, what the old preacher told William Carey concerning his missionary dreams and ambitions, "Sit down, Young Man; when God is pleased to convert the heathen, He will do it without your aid, or mine." Packer correctly commented that we should "think twice before you condemn that old man" because he had, in fact, "learned to take the sovereignty of God perfectly seriously. His mistake was that he was not taking the church's evangelistic responsibility with equal seriousness."

The second story concerns Charles Haddon Spurgeon's answer to the question of how he could "reconcile" the truths of God's sovereignty and human responsibility. "I wouldn't try," he answered; "I never reconcile friends."[32]

John had been a Christian less than a year. He had his fellow workers at the paper mill on his heart. In his zeal to witness to them he had sometimes provoked some unkind criticism. One night he said to the president of the men's organization in his church, "You know, Sam, I don't know where to turn; Nathan has been one of my best friends for years, but he seems to be on the defensive all the time. If I say a word to him about the Lord, or even the church, he always comes up with something like, 'Well, I think religion is something everybody has to work out for himself. I don't think people ought to be talking to other people about their religion.' Then I was talking to another guy about it and he said, 'You have to let the Spirit lead. You don't want to sin against the Holy Spirit. So maybe you'd better cool it.' What is it the Bible says about the Spirit doing the convicting, and what is it about waiting for the power?"

The above conversation between John and Sam had occurred where several of the men were involved in a work project in a house the church had just bought for a clothes closet and mission Bible study classes in a deprived community. Sam's answer to John was, "I believe you got one for the Reverend there. I know the Bible talks about all those things, but I believe he could give you better help than I can."

"Gary," Sam said to the bi-vocational pastor at coffee break, "I think Johnnie has a little theological problem for you."

"What's the problem, Johnnie?" Gary asked, as he moved his coffee cup around beside John. They looked together at Luke 24:49: "And behold, I send the promise of my Father

56 Evangelism for All God's People

upon you; but stay in the city, until you are clothed with power from on high." Gary explained that these words of Jesus were spoken before the events of the Day of Pentecost recorded in Acts 2 and that Jesus was likely telling the disciples to expect the great empowering experience. He explained that after Pentecost they were no longer told to wait, as the Holy Spirit was already present in them. They then read John 16:8, "And when he (the Holy Spirit) comes he will convince the world concerning sin and righteousness and judgment . . ."

Gary explained that no person can experience salvation unless the Spirit convinces or convicts the sinner of sin, but that very likely the Holy Spirit always accompanies the presentation of the Word, and we don't have to wait on God to do his work, because God is more interested in people than we are.

Gary then went on patiently to explain to John that we are ambassadors for Christ (2 Cor. 5:20) and that an ambassador is always very diplomatic in trying to respect the other person's personality and sense of self-worth, and that, even though the Holy Spirit is ready and God's power is available, we have to be careful in timing and approaches just like we do when talking with people about any other matter. He even gave him an illustration about how he (the pastor) had found it necessary to back off for awhile from witnessing to someone, but soon another friend took the man to a ball game, invited him and his wife out for a snack after the game, and had a good chance to witness to them both, resulting in the wife beginning to attend services. She has since been baptized and the husband is attending services regularly.

"You see, Johnnie, the Holy Spirit uses His Word and our patient, consistent presentation. Why don't we have a prayer for Nathan right now?" After the prayer the pastor assured John that very likely he or some other person will have an

opportunity to be used of the Spirit in leading his friend to the
Lord.

The Evangelist and Conversion

The Acts record reveals several characteristics about conversions in the early church. First, as already indicated, God
was the initiator. The Holy Spirit was clearly in charge at
Pentecost. He performed a miracle at the temple gate
(Acts 3). The Holy Spirit provided boldness in the face of
threats (4:31). The number of conversions was phenomenal
beyond human explanation (4:4; 6:7; 9:31; 11:21,24). The
quality of human lives was changed, as illustrated in Saul of
Tarsus. God was the only explanation.

A second inescapable characteristic of early Christian conversions is the place of person participation. The leaders
modeled human participation: Peter at Pentecost (Acts 1 and
2), Peter and John at the temple gate, Peter and John in their
encouragement to Philip in Samaria, and their evangelistic
ministry on their return to Jerusalem, Peter in Lydda and
Sharon (9:32-35), Peter at Joppa (9:42) and the well-known
story of Peter's visit with Cornelius and others in Caesarea
(Ch. 10). Paul was a model in helping people "turn to the
Lord" from Antioch on (14:15; 26:18,20) throughout his in-
comparable ministry. No doubt other apostles demonstrated
similar dedication to helping persons know Jesus in the conversion experience.

Let's look into the ministry of some we would likely classify
as "lay people" (while admitting those distinctions are not
clear in the New Testament). Barnabas is a case in point.
During the early years of my Christian journey I met, heard,
and read Dr. J. G. Hughes, who was a pastor in Kingsport
and Memphis and president of the Tennessee Baptist Convention.[33] Hughes, who preached and wrote about Barnabas,

was convinced he was a "layman." I recall that one of his strongest arguments was that Barnabas owned real estate and was willing to give some of it to the use of the Lord (Acts 4:36-37). Were both the "owning" and "giving" unpreacher-like characteristics? Barnabas, known as "Mr. Encouragement," must have been Exhibit A in relational evangelism. He not only was encourager to Saul (9:27) and Mark (15:39) but personally participated in helping people be "added to the Lord" (11:24).

Stephen and Philip were among the laymen selected to serve tables (6:1*ff*), but immediately we see them actively participating in the communication of the gospel (Chs. 7, 8). At the time of the persecution of Saul, participation in communication of the gospel seems to have been widespread among all believers (8:1,4). Do you suppose that Ananias, who witnessed to Saul, and Philip, who ministered to the Ethiopian, represented a much larger group of believers who were behaving similarly? Wouldn't it seem normal aside from our present-day perversion of participation? These were laypersons!

Paul certainly made clear the divine *and* human factors in conversions:

> Therefore, if anyone is in Christ, he is a new creation; the old has passed away, behold, the new has come. All this is from God, who through Christ reconciled us to himself and gave us the ministry of reconciliation; that is, God was in Christ reconciling the world unto himself, not counting their trespasses against them, and entrusting to us the message of reconciliation. So we are ambassadors for Christ, God making his appeal through us (2 Cor. 5:17-20).

All God's people are under authority to proclaim the good news. We are to "make disciples" as we go from place to place and from person to person (Matt. 28:18-20). The main means of conversion in the early church was communication of the good news. The Gentiles were converted as they heard and believed (Acts 15:7). Paul was very clear that the gospel is not the gospel until it is heard (Rom. 10:14). So we have discussed "God and Conversion," "The Evangelist and Conversion," and now we come to the third important person in the "turning to God" process, "the hearer and conversion."

The Hearer and Conversion

It is essential that the marketplace evangelist keep objectives in perspective. The goal is not to satisfy one's own ego or do one's duty. It coincides with the purpose of Jesus in coming into the world: "that they may have life" (John 10:10); "to seek and to save the lost" (Luke 19:10). So since the goal in communicating the gospel to a person is "a new creation" (2 Cor. 5:17); "mature manhood, to the measure of the stature of the fullness of Christ" (Eph. 4:13), we will now examine the conversion experience from the standpoint of the hearer, what he needs, and how to help him receive it.

We have discussed the good news of Jesus' death and resurrection (1 Cor. 15:3) against the background of bad news (Rom. 3:23; 5:12) of sin in the lives of all people. How does the hearer respond to the good news? God offers reconciliation through Christ. We deliver the message of reconciliation. The Holy Spirit convicts of sin, righteousness, and judgment. The hearer must respond.

Repentance

How? Following Peter's Pentecostal sermon the people asked, "What shall we do? (Acts 2:37). Peter's answer was, "repent, and be baptized . . . in the name of Jesus Christ, for the forgiveness of your sins." Jesus had said, "Repent, and believe in the gospel" (Mark 1:15).

A lawyer, while working on a brief, knocked on the door of a senior member of the firm who was known to be an active Christian and asked, pen and note pad in hand, "Tom, in religious parlance, what does *repent* mean?"

The prisoner was looking through the bars at the Gideon who was visiting the jail. "What do I do when I repent?" she asked. In New Testament usage repentance *(metanoia)* means a change of mind, or purpose, or point of view. It carries the idea of a new judgment with regret and sorrow for past action or thought. Repentance is the awakened awareness of past sin.[34]

Dr. Stagg wrote:

> The call to 'repentance,' then, was a call to *persons* for a radical turn from one way of life to another. In effect it was a call to *conversion* from self-love, self-trust, and self-assertion to the way of obedient trust and self-commitment to God in Christ as sovereign.[35]

A. H. Strong defines repentance as a "voluntary change in the mind of the sinner in which he turns from sin." He defines it in terms of three elements: (1) An intellectual element—a change of view; (2) An emotional element—a change of feeling; and (3) A voluntary element—a change of purpose.[36]

It should also be pointed out that repentance is possible because of the work of God's Spirit. Jesus produces repentance just as He does forgiveness (Acts 5:31; 11:18; Romans 2:4; 2 Timothy 2:25). Repentance is a gift of God, yet it is not coerced. God provides it but does not impose it. "Man cannot achieve but only receive repentance, yet he must receive it." "There is no conversion without repentance.

The Lordship of Christ is involved in repentance and the

total conversion experience. Once while working on some material for counseling converts I asked Dr. William Coble, professor of New Testament at Midwestern Baptist Theological Seminary, for some help in explaining what happens when a person is converted.[37] He wisely pointed out that one of the most important elements, and most overlooked, is the lordship of Christ. When one turns from self as lord, he turns to the Lord Christ to become lord of life. How old must we be to become a Christian? We must be old enough to repent of sin, which would assume a knowledge of sin, and to make Christ Lord of life.

Faith

Another essential requirement in conversion is *belief* (see Acts 4:4; 8:12; 9:42; 11:21; 13:12; 14:1; 16:30-31; 17:2,34; 19:18). Paul quoted Joel, "Everyone who calls upon the name of the Lord will be saved" and then asked, "but how are men to call upon him in whom they have not believed?" (Rom. 10:13-14).

The English word *believe* isn't quite an accurate translation of the Greek. *Faith* is a better word but the English does not have a verb "to faith." The idea is confidence and trust. A person not only believes that Jesus is the Son of God and Savior, but is willing to commit his life to Christ. You have faith in the doctor, so you put your life in his hands. You believe that Jesus is the Christ, you know you need Him, so you commit your whole being to Him to give you new and eternal life. Furthermore, you are not merely trusting Him only to put your name in the book to assure you of heaven when you die, but to take over your life now with all its components: personal, family, vocation, recreation, entertainment, relationships, as well as church work.

Commitment

So when you lead a person to conversion you lead that person to commit all of life, forever. He does not merely get under the umbrella for protection. She or he becomes a new person (2 Cor. 5:17) with allegiance to a new kingdom. It is a binding commitment to a new Lord, daily and forever, in everything.

Once when I was preaching in India I asked Pastor Sampath, "What should I keep in mind especially as I try to witness to people with a Hindu background, particularly the high caste Brahman Hindus?"[38] He said,

> Two things: First, you make clear that Christianity is not just another religion they can put under the umbrella. To receive Christ is to reject all other gods. Second, emphasize the personal relationship one can enjoy with Christ. They need to know that Christ knows them personally, loves them personally, fellowships with them, and will answer the prayers of individual Christians.[39]

It should also be said emphatically at this point that conversion is not committing oneself to the culture of some particular social group, country, or civilization. An African convert does not become a Korean, an Indian does not become English, a Chinese convert does not become an American. Neither is it assumed that a new convert in Toronto will take on the mores and culture of the rural Southern United States.

A Christian convert is a new creation in Christ Jesus and is obligated to Christ and His kingdom. Culture is involved only to the point that it affects one's sinful life before new life in Christ. Every culture has something to contribute to all other cultures but in cross-cultural evangelism it is no more necessary for our convert to adopt our culture than it is for an American to adopt the culture of ancient Palestine.

In a real sense evangelism is telling another person how to become a Christian. It is not necessary to become a theologian but it is necessary to understand the basic, scriptural, Spirit-empowered, experience of turning from sin and self in faith to God through Christ. Jesus would not have commanded every Christian to participate in evangelism if it were not possible and necessary for every Christian to participate in evangelism.

The essential message of the evangelist is that God's love has provided for human salvation. Because all have sinned, the price for sin is death. Christ died for our sins, was raised from the dead, and assures us that if we will place our faith and trust in Him, He will let His death count for our sin, will set us free from the law of sin and death, and by His resurrection raise us up to become new creatures in Christ Jesus.

2
Biblical Foundations of Evangelism

The People of God in the Old Testament

God desired a people to fellowship with him, worship, and serve him. He said, "Let us make man in our image, after our likeness . . . So God created man in his own image, in the image of God created he him." (Gen. 1:26,27). Obviously, to be a person capable of worship, fellowship, and service, God's creation had to be capable of deciding about his relationships, even those with God. God gave him a lot of latitude, even the choice to decide whether he would obey and serve God or try to control his own life, as his own god. The full life and latitude given him depended, of course, upon his relationship with God. If he chose to live independently of God, he would be without the total life that God had provided. All people broke the relationship and wasted the full and meaningful life God was providing. God's purposes were dissipated and human potential gambled away (see Gen. 2:15-17; 3:6-7).

Before Abraham

But God, praise His name, did not give up. He kept reaching out to reclaim and restore. There is the touching human interest story of Adam and Eve's embarrassment in each

other's presence after they had sinned. But read the electrify-
ing words that follow:

> And they heard the sound of the Lord God walking in the
> garden in the cool of the day, and the man and his wife hid
> themselves from the presence of the Lord among the trees of
> the garden. But the Lord God called to the man, and said to
> him, "Where are you?" (Gen. 3:7-9)

God was reaching out in love. Look at another love-bathed
question: Following Cain's murder of his brother Abel, the
Lord asked, "Where is your brother?" (4:9) The implications
are that the love from God and for God cannot be divorced
from love for others. God was reaching out in love.

God's desire for fellowship with those created in His image
and after His likeness is gracefully illustrated in the brief but
spiritually stimulating story of Enoch (5:21-24). The writer of
Hebrews emphasized the pleasure of God in fellowship and
used the experience to illustrate how such love produces human love (Heb. 11:5-6). God was reaching out in love.

God's compassionate love was strikingly demonstrated in
the story of Noah. Even though human sin demanded divine
judgment, God's love would not allow His people to be lost
from Him. He used the most righteous and obedient, though
not perfect, person He had as an agent of salvation (Genesis
6—9). God was reaching out in love.

The people at Shinar repeated the spirit of Adam and Eve
in defying God for the purpose of making themselves invinci-
ble by building the tower of Babel. The confusion of tongues
was a redemptive act in behalf of His people (Genesis 11:
1-9). The scattered people foreshadowed God's love for the
nations He would call Israel to bless. God was reaching out
in love before Abraham. The story of human rejection had
already begun. God had created people in His image with

extraordinary capacities and potential. The results were disappointing. He provided freedom and they chose slavery. He provided salvation. They chose sin. He desired fellowship, but they chose estrangement. But God kept reaching out in love.

Abraham

The story of Abraham is a story of God's outreach for a people. Abraham is not only "father" to Hebrew and Moslem religions, but assuredly to Christians as well. One could not sit in the classes of the late J. McKee Adams, professor of biblical backgrounds in The Southern Baptist Theological Seminary, Louisville, Kentucky, without beginning a lifetime of deep emotional response to the very words, "Father Abraham." He promised his students, "We will walk where Father Abraham walked." We did.[40] You can understand Abraham's distinction among Old Testament characters better when you are reminded that Abraham is mentioned nearly half as much in the New Testament as in the Old.

God and Abraham

To begin talking or writing about Abraham is to discover you cannot begin talking or writing about Abraham. It is like approaching the door of a building only to face a warning; "Use other entrance, please." To talk about Abraham you have to begin with God. God's call to Abraham transcends human explanation. Wherever you read about Abraham you read about the sovereignty of God. Stephen, one of the seven "laymen" brought in to minister with the apostles (Acts 6:1*ff*), was brought before the council because of his boldness. In his defense he said,

> Brethren, fathers, hear me. The God of glory appeared to our father Abraham . . . and said to him, "Depart from your

land and from your kindred and go into the land which I will show you." Then he departed from the land of the Chaldeans, and lived in Haran (Acts 7:2-4).

Listen to another testimony, "By faith Abraham obeyed when he was called to go out to a place which he was to receive as an inheritance; and he went out, not knowing where he was to go" (Heb. 11:8).

Look for the initiative of God in his original call to Abraham:

> Now the Lord said to Abram, "Go from your country and from your kindred and your father's house to the land that I will show you. And I will make of you a great nation, and I will bless you, and make your name great, so that you will be a blessing. I will bless those who bless you, and him who curses you I will curse; and by you all the families of the earth shall bless themselves [or shall be blessed]" (Gen. 12:1-3).

So the first thing you see in the story of Abraham is the sovereignty of God.

Second, you see the purpose of God. His purpose was clear in creation. His purpose to have a people was clear in all His pre-Abrahamic people relationships. The revelation of that purpose is even more clearly defined in Abraham's call and throughout his remarkable life. The importance of this doctrine cannot be overemphasized. An insurance salesman (who became an insurance executive) gave the following testimony: "I was pretty stubborn about being willing to assume any responsibility about other people's relationship with God until I realized one day that this was God's purpose for my life, and that of all his people. When I truly heard Jesus say, 'As the Father has sent me, even so I send you' (John 20:21), I knew he was sending me to all the people I see every day in my business, and everywhere else."

In the third place, God's calling and direction in Abraham's life emphasizes God's doctrine of election. I remember hearing about election in the country church I attended as a child.[41] At first I thought the preacher's "annual call" by the church was what he was talking about. When I found out that was not what he was talking about, I heard him saying that some people were called to be saved and some were called to be forever lost. Sure enough then, I heard Mr. Perry, our deacon neighbor, say to Papa, "I believe Brother _____ is more a 'Hardshell' Baptist than a 'Missionary' Baptist." As I recall I thought of "election" as a heresy until I got to college and heard the religion professor explain that election is God's purpose and provision for man's salvation. Somewhere during those early years I heard someone define God's doctrine of election as God's plan to save the largest possible number of people in the shortest possible time. Not bad. You see in our passage (Gen. 12:3*ff*) that God selected, elected, and called Abraham "to be a blessing" and promised that through him "all the families of the earth would be a blessing."

Frequently you get the idea that many people have the mistaken notion that Abraham and his descendants, the Israelites, were the chosen people just in order that they might be blessed of God. There is no question that He blessed them — but it is very clear that He blessed them in order that they might "be a blessing" to all nations. We are elected for salvation, though God does not force it upon us. We are elected to serve others, though God will not force us to do it. God calls but does not coerce.

The fourth clear characteristic of God in the call of Abraham is His trust in people. Once in a class a student raised the question, "Did God take a risk in calling Abraham?" Another student answered, "Yes, just like He takes a chance with you and me. If we don't obey Him, He will have to call someone else to do what He has called us to do." Then inevitably, another student added, "We don't know how many better ones turned Him down before He ever resorted to call us." And then because there is more than one in every class, still another student fired back at the last one, "If your wife could have had who she wanted she probably never would have gotten to you."

A fifth point of interest in God's relations with Abraham is the fact that He took Abraham into His confidence. He revealed to Abraham His plan to destroy Sodom and Gomorrah (Gen. 18:17*ff*). This is closely related to what has been said about trust, but it is another reminder that God depends heavily upon His people. So a long time before Paul wrote about our being ambassadors for Christ it is clear that Abraham was God's ambassador in His world. There seems to be no evidence that Abraham's calling from God had any more to do with his method of making a living than would be true with a godly banker, businessman, politician, or farmer. However, there was no doubt of his calling.

Why Abraham?

It would be as difficult to explain why God called Abraham as would be true of Moses, David, Isaiah, Saul of Tarsus, or Billy Graham. On the negative side, he had no orientation in the kind of religion in which he would become a world leader for all time. He was from Ur of the Chaldees, a people of moon-god worshippers. He probably was unfamiliar with monotheistic worship, much less any knowledge of the God he was to follow. As is true with other biblical characters, the Bible does not present a perfect picture of Abraham. He failed the integrity test on more than one occasion. When going into Egypt he instructed Sarai to lie to the Egyptians about her true identity. She was a beautiful woman and he was afraid they would kill him and keep her if they knew she was his wife. So he told her to say she was his sister. He repeated the same lie with King Abimelech of Gerar.

Both of these moral defections grew out of a lack of faith, which was, after all, the best thing he had going for him. He was not willing to trust God to protect him and Sarai. Another illustration of his lack of faith caused him a lot of trouble over the years. He did not offer, so far as we know, any resistance to Sarai's suggestion that her maid be the mother of his child. Then later when God tried to assure him that Sarah—her name had been changed along with his change from Abram to Abraham—would mother the promised heir, he virtually said to God, "I don't believe you but I will strike a deal with you. Why not let Ishmael be my heir" (Gen. 17:18 TEV, author's paraphrase)? One businessman, in a discussion of "mission in the marketplace," said, "I guess most of us laymen just don't think we are quite good enough for that kind of ministry." Maybe Abraham raised that question, too.

On the positive side, Abraham's life compares admirably with any and all who live this side of Sinai, or for that matter, with the church age. He appropriately received more space than anybody else in God's Hall of Fame (Heb. 11). It was all based upon his obedient faith, the first requirement for all God's people who will serve Him as ministers. His faith was the basis for his obedience, whether in leaving his people and country or offering his son as a sacrifice. God's promise to Abraham and Abraham's faith were at the heart of God's outreach of love to the rest of the world until Jesus came. He continues to minister through the Word and will until Jesus comes again.

Joseph

One day I asked a professor of Old Testament to think of Old Testament leaders within the framework of our contemporary notions of clergy and laymen, and name me some outstanding laymen.[42] The first name he gave me was Joseph. We are all familiar with his story as the favorite son of Jacob and what that favoritism cost Joseph in suffering during the early years of his life. Horatio Alger, Jr., famous hero novelist of my boyhood years, never in his wildest imagination, came up with a better success story. Furthermore, the Bible never tells of a more flawless life, always lived in obedience and honor to his God. He was a "lay minister" *par excellence.* Certainly no person between Abraham and Moses compares with both of them so favorably.

Moses and the Exodus

The film industry vis a vis Charlton Heston in Cecil B. De-Mille's 1956 classic *The Ten Commandments* has helped to make Moses a folk hero in our generation, along with the biblical record and Jewish national history. However, Christians of all ages have always honored him as having been a giant among ministers of God through all the centuries of human history. Adults, as well as children, have enjoyed the story of baby Moses. There is clear evidence that the hand of God was upon him and he was being divinely groomed for God's ministry. Without a doubt his early life in the king's house was part of God's plan of preparation. Could it have been God's plan for him to lead Israel out of Egyptian bondage from the vantage point of the king's house, had he not acted impulsively in killing the Egyptian? Would it have saved decades of time and bitter suffering? Who knows? Aren't all our lives filled with "might have beens"? However

God might have done it otherwise, but He used the Midian experience as a part of Moses' preparation for his major life assignment.

The Divine Call

There can be no question that God called Moses into His ministry. From the moment of the burning bush Moses was involved in "full-time ministry." There can be no doubt that some are thus called. This does not answer the question as to whether some are called later in life or only respond later. It does not answer the question as to whether all who are called to give all their time to "priestly ministries" are called to do so for the rest of their lives. Perhaps it is the part of godly wisdom to avoid trying to fence God in.

Moses, along with Joseph, is another Old Testament illustration of God's call to some to be leaders. To be called is to be gifted and empowered. Also special training is usually required. To be called, gifted, empowered, and trained is not to be manipulative, or authoritarian; but it is to be strong, courageous, bold, and often self-sacrificing. God evidently does not call some to usurp the rights and personhoods of others, but He does call some to be teachers, leaders, organizers, equippers, and enablers, by the power of God's Spirit. Gaines S. Dobbins, dean of church administration leaders, used to talk about "first among equals." It is not that "some are more equal than others."

Moses was sometimes impulsive and fractious, and paid for it dearly, but there is no doubt that he is one of God's greatest leadership role models. We are familiar with Moses' struggles with Pharaoh, and also his own people, but we will look at some of the evidences that God was preparing a people for ministry in the world, just as He had indicated to Abraham in his call.

The Sinai Revival (Ex. 19:2-9)

Everything that lives seems to need occasional revival. Springtime is a revival in nature; the big sale, or even merger, may be necessary revival in business; a change in leadership may provide for revival in government; and we seem to need repeated and continuous spiritual revival. In the wilderness of Sinai, God was preparing to give the "law" as a necessary instructional and disciplinary guide for all His people for all time. Before giving the Decalogue to Moses on tables of stone, God led the people in a revival of awareness of their role in history, and then in a consecration of themselves to Him. Amid the awesome surroundings, God's presence was verified as He called to Moses "out of the mountain."

First, God reminded them of who they were: "say to the house of Jacob and tell the people of Israel." Second, of how He had blessed them, just as he had promised Abraham: "You have seen what I did to the Egyptians, and how I bore you on eagles' wings." (See Deut. 32:11-12, a description of how the parent eagle teaches its young to fly.) Third, He gave them the conditions of future blessings and ministry. "*If* you will obey my voice and keep my covenant." Fourth, He defined more clearly Israel's relationship as the people of God: "you shall be my own possession among all peoples" (NASB).

In addition to their larger possessions as kings, ancient political leaders had their own "special treasures" they guarded in a special way. Remember Israel was blessed to be a blessing. He went on to remind them of His concern for all people: "all the earth is mine," but "you shall be to me a kingdom of priests and a holy nation." Israel was to be God's ambassador and representative, His messenger and priest to all the people of the world. His relationship with them as priests was exclusive so that His relationship with the world could be inclusive.

Following the spiritual renewal, or as part of it, God gave the Ten Commandments, which were to be the heart of Judaism and the custodial tutor for Christians. So you see the strategic importance of the Sinai revival for all the people of God until the close of the age. It was so important that God continued His reminders to them repeatedly. They would renew their vows and fail again (Ex. 24:3; 32:7-14; Josh. 24:1-28; Judg. 2:11—4:3; 1 Kings 9:1-9; 18:20-24,38-40; 19:15-18).

The Hebrew Songs

Even the music of the people of God was used by Him to remind them of their worldwide responsibility. He told them that the Lord has control of the nations (Ps. 2:8). They were told to tell the people (9:11). They were reminded of the worldwide nature of God's concern (22:27-28). The Lord continued through the Psalms to try to inspire His people in evangelism (47:7-9; 57:9; 67:1-5, 96:3; 117:1-2; 145:18-21; 150:6).

The Prophets

God kept repeating through the prophets the stewardship responsibility of Israel to the rest of the world:

1. Amos in the first two chapters mentioned Damascus, Gaza (Philistia), Tyre (Phoenicia), Edom, Ammon, and Moab.

2. Hosea spoke with deep conviction and daring clarity, making himself and his family vulnerable.

3. Micah brought a similar message to that of Amos and Hosea, except with more optimism. He portrays a remnant working among many peoples.

4. The most evangelistically inspiring of the Old Testament prophets is Jonah.

5. The best known evangelism messages are to be found in Isaiah (compare 2:2-4 with Mic. 4:1-3). Other familiar passages: 9:2-7; 11:1-10; 19:19-22; 34:1-4; 40:12-26; 42:1-4; 43:8-13; 44:6-20; 49:1-7.

6. Other prophets with a worldwide message are Jeremiah, Habakkuk, Joel, Ezekiel, Zechariah, and Malachi.

There is no doubt that God called Abraham to be the father of a people, God's people, to represent Him to the nations of the earth. Before we criticize the Israelites too harshly we need to review Christian history. Before we deal too harshly with Christian history we need to review what all the Christian groups of the world are doing today, with all the advantages of technology, communication, and missionary organizations, or rather, what we are *not* doing.* *

The People of God in the New Testament

Galatians 4:4 describes the coming of Jesus as in the "fullness of (the) time (KJV)." It is no accident that the history of the gospel of Jesus Christ had its beginning in the same place and time that was significant in the history of the Roman Empire and its development.[43]

Streams of history, politics, economics, and religion converged to comprise a mighty river that changed the course of mankind for time and eternity. Christianity emerged out of a people who had intense religious awareness of themselves as the elect of God; as a nation of God's own people. God had given them their land and their proud heritage. But changes came to the Jewish nation.

With the victory at Actium in 31 B.C. the Roman Empire

* *I wish to express gratitude to my former teacher Dr. H. C. Goerner for his class lectures and his book *Thus It Is Written* (Convention Press, 1944).

began to solidify and flex its muscles. Emperor Augustus came to power. He conquered Philippi, settled Romans in it, and granted the city the privileges of Roman citizenship subject only to the laws of the imperial government in Rome. Augustus marched through the land ever widening Rome's circle of control. Caesar Augustus incorporated the Holy Land into his empire in A.D. 6 and sent officials into the land to rule it. He placed the region on a secure foundation and ushered them into the larger *Pax Romana*. But the Jews did not accept his rule graciously. Augustus had to face uprisings spurred on by the Zealots during his establishment of the Roman Empire in the Holy Land. But the revolts of the Zealots could not stand against the armies of Caesar. Rebellions were crushed.

An unparalleled time of peace and security came to the empire. According to many scholars Augustus Caesar, who was Caesar when Jesus was born (Luke 2:1), was not only the ablest of the emperors but ranked as one of the greatest statesmen in history.[44]

Rome became a great city under Augustus's leadership. Commerce flourished. The famous Roman roads were built. The wild Mediterranean Sea, plagued by pirates, was conquered by government ships. Over this body of water ships sailed back and forth keeping the empire in constant touch with all its outposts. Also, over these waters the apostle Paul found freedom of travel to carry the gospel into major cities in the empire.

The most important contribution the Romans made was in the establishment of government. The Romans brought stability with their unique form of government. The Roman model of an Emperor and a Senate has been copied many times through history. The Senate, composed of prominent leaders, served as a check on the power of the Emperor.

However, the Emperor had the power to remove any Senator, therefore, in effect he was absolute in his authority. But the combination of Senate and Emperor gave stability to the form of government.

One important concept the Romans brought to conquered territories was that of letting conquered people retain their own local laws and customs as long as they did not interfere with Roman laws.[45] The New Testament reflects this custom regarding the punishment and crucifixion of Jesus. The Jews brought Jesus to the Romans to crucify Him. At one point in his examination Pilate, who was governor of the region, sought to release Jesus into the hands of the Jews so they might exercise their own laws over Jesus (John 18:31ff). But as John 18:31ff indicates, the Jews had to refer all capital offenses to Roman law. Even at the last Pilate tried to get out from under the conflict between Jewish custom and Roman law by setting one prisoner free. To his amazement the Jews condemned Jesus.

Although there were cases that required Rome's intervention, for the most part the Jews handled their affairs according to their own laws. In some instances, the territories even retained their own rulers. The people were subject to Rome and had to pay taxes as the New Testament indicates (Matt. 22:17-22). But the overall policy of letting the conquered people rule themselves lessened for each conquered territory the burden of being a conquered people.

Rome existed as the center of Roman rule but Jerusalem was the most important city for the Jews. Its importance was felt in every way. To Jerusalem came merchants from all over the world, especially from Judea and all Palestine. Jerusalem was a busy city full of trade and commerce. It was also the political hub for all Jewish politics. As we have learned, the Romans let the Jews keep their religious customs as long as they did not conflict with Roman law in any way. Jerusalem was not only an ancient city with history that every Jewish child learned, but was the center of all activity regarding religious ceremony and festivals as well as the seat of authority in all religious matters. This was because the Sanhedrin sat in Jerusalem.

There was a strange mix of life in Jerusalem at the time of Jesus. Jerusalem was the old capital city. Strangers came to the city for religious festivals but also because of the culture and politics there, but also because of what Herod, the procurator of the region, brought there.

Herod's court was there. According to the scholar Joachim Jeremias, Herod brought Roman games, music, gymnastics, chariot races, and theater to Jerusalem.[46] Foreigners took an active part in the contests of the day. Ambassadors, messengers, and foreign leaders came to Jerusalem. Herod's court was a powerful magnet that attracted the world to Jerusalem.

Because of the presence of the Sanhedrin in Jerusalem all religious authority was focused on the city. The Sanhedrin had great influence over the people. In fact, Acts 9:2 tells of Paul's letters to the Synagogue at Damascus which contained orders to seize Christians there and deliver them to the Sanhedrin in Jerusalem.

After A.D. 6 when the Romans came to power in Jerusalem, the Sanhedrin's greatest influence was felt. It served not only as the religious authority for Judea and the Jews but became the chief political agent for the Romans into the affairs of the Jews. According to Jeremias, "A committee of the Sanhedrin was in charge of finance in the eleven Jewish toparchies into which the Romans had divided the land."[47] Thus, every little village had links with Jerusalem because of the influence of the Sanhedrin.

Jerusalem was also the center of religious education. Scholars from all over the world came there to study. Zealots focused their attention on Jerusalem as they tried to usher in the kingdom of God through their guerilla tactics. The Essenes and other groups located near there. Christians made Jerusalem their capital city as is indicated by the gifts that were sent from as far away as Macedonia to aid the church there. People aspired to die in Jerusalem. In fact, the language of the New Testament indicates its importance when it speaks of, "going down from Jerusalem." All other localities whether higher in actual elevation above sea level or not were "down" from Jerusalem. After being in Jerusalem, there was no higher plane.

Most important of all in Jerusalem was the temple. It was the grand symbol of God's presence with his people. It was Herod's gift to the nation. Here men came to pray. To the temple they brought sacrifices. To the temple they brought a temple tax. To the temple came the priests. And three times a year all Jewry made a pilgrimage there. The press of the crowds was apparent. Roman guards controlled the crowds in large numbers. Josephus wrote that in A.D. 70 when Jerusalem was destroyed during Passover as many as 1,200,000 were trapped in the city at the time of siege.[48] No doubt the pilgrims who came to Jerusalem three times a year represented a staggering number. One can only imagine the scene of Jesus riding into the city in triumphal procession during His last Passover.

Into such a culture and world was Jesus of Nazareth born. Certainly, it was in the fullness of time. Politically, economically, spiritually and culturally, the time was right. The planting of the gospel of Christ came to fertile soil and sprang to flower in one of the most pivotal eras in world history.

Jesus of Nazareth

Jesus was born in Bethlehem and then raised in the small town of Nazareth. We now celebrate this little town, but before his birth, it was just a typical small village nestled in the region of Galilee.[49] The population of Galilee was mixed. Phoenicians, Syrians, Arabs and Greeks lived in the country. Therefore, Jesus would grow into a culture where He would be used to people of many colors.

Jesus was born under the reign of Augustus who was often referred to as "the savior of the world." Jesus' name was given to him, as Scripture says, "because he would save his people." The New Testament writers were careful to show who the *real* savior of the world was. Jesus was a very common name in that day.[50] The writers of the New Testament wanted to separate Him from all others who bore this name. They were careful to call him Christ, Lord, and Messiah (Acts 2:36).

Jesus' father and mother were laborers. No doubt the home was one of simplicity but not poverty due to the carpentry trade that Joseph practiced.[51] In that day due to the simplicity of life, most people were similar in their life-style.[52] Even today, vast numbers of people in the East live very simple lifestyles, far removed from the complicated life-style of the West.

Jesus was educated like most boys of his day. He learned to read and write by rote memory. That is, he repeated what he was taught until he knew the contents by heart. In small Jewish towns the schoolmaster was the *hazzan* or reader in the synagogue.[53] So, Jesus probably grew up memorizing vast numbers of Old Testament passages and passages from other sacred writings of the synagogue.

Not much is known about the youth of Jesus. We can only guess that he was raised like most of the youth of his day. He no doubt knew little of the Roman way of life and may not have known its language, Greek. He was close to the small village life of Nazareth and to nature. Many of his parables reflect His love of simplicity and nature.

Jesus was no professional, trained theologian as were the Pharisees of his day. He was simply a by-product of a strict Jewish home and the culture of a small town in the Galilean countryside. But he had a sensitivity to God that was unique. With such a background, He began His ministry around the age of thirty, which was the age that reflected maturity in men of His day. As he ventured into the countryside He saw his cousin, John the Baptizer, a charismatic figure that many came to hear.

Jesus and John the Baptist

John the Baptist was an itinerant evangelist who seemed to be in the tradition of the prophets of old. His manner of dress and message seemed to reflect not only urgency but action as well. Little is known about John except he is seen as the announcer of the Messiah to come.

John associated his preaching with an urgency marked by the words, "repent and be baptized for the remission of sins." His baptism was unlike the baptism taught at Qumran. At Qumran, baptism was a repeated act that was supposed to wash away sins, much like a moral cleansing. John's baptism was not that. It was a unique baptism that came as a result of a change of heart.

John associated his baptism with the coming of the Kingdom of God. When that day came, the one who repented would submit to it. John never saw that the Kingdom of God rested on his shoulders. It was to come and he was to announce it. To John came crowds of people who wished to participate in his baptism. For many who heard John, no doubt it was an effort on their part to continue in the mode of expectation related to the coming of the Messiah and the desire on the part of many of the humble to be ready for it.

Jesus came to John to be baptized. No doubt Jesus had observed the preaching of John for days or weeks. He had heard the stirring messages. Some scholars have debated why Jesus chose to be baptized by John. That discussion is beyond the scope of this work. Suffice it to say that the New Testament records the event as the launching of Jesus' personal ministry. Jesus may have wanted to affirm John's messages which were a stern call for moral renewal, and for a fresh start that the kingdom of God required.[54]

But there was a difference between the understanding and preaching of John and Jesus regarding the kingdom of God. John believed that it would be ushered in when people repented and when as with the Old Testament prophets, the terrible Day of the Lord dawned. Jesus announced the Kingdom of God was here already. Jesus also required people to repent but also to believe in Him and the good news He was preaching. John never told people to trust in his gospel. Jesus announced that with Him the Kingdom had dawned.

Jesus and the Kingdom of God

The term *Kingdom of God* was a favorite of Jesus. But it meant much more than most of his hearers understood. Most of His hearers no doubt understood the term to mean the reign of God within Judaism. To the Zealot it would mean the overthrow of the Romans. To Jesus it meant the worship, honor, and reign of the one true God of their fathers in the lives of the people.

The Sermon on the Mount reflects Jesus' understanding of

those who would live lives where God's voice would be the prime motivator for them. Those who would partake of the Kingdom of God would be those who were not obsessed with self but rather would be controlled by Christ in everything. With that message Jesus began His ministry.

Jesus — the Evangelist

Jesus began His work of evangelism with a plan. His plan was people, specifically, the disciples. Jesus did not gather His disciples from a group of people who wished to study under a formal teacher. Rather, His disciples were men who followed Him because they loved Him, were fascinated by Him, and who wanted to identify with Him.

Jesus went to Capernaum to launch His ministry with His disciples. This area became a favored spot for Him. He immediately struck up an acquaintance with two brothers, Simon and Andrew. Both were successful fishermen in Capernaum when Jesus met them.

Peter was married and lived with his family and mother-in-law. Andrew may have been a disciple of John the Baptist. At least he appears to have been a searcher for the truth (John 1:40). It was with ordinary laypersons that Jesus sought to establish His kingdom. In fact, it appears that even while they were following Jesus, they continued to apply their trade (Matt. 4:18, Mark 1:16). What a picture of evangelism in the marketplace! They followed Jesus, helped Him proclaim His message, and worked at their nets.

Another family befriended Jesus — the family of Zebedee, a well-to-do fisherman.[55] He owned several boats and always gave Jesus a warm welcome. His two sons, James the elder and John were committed disciples. Salome, the wife of Zebedee stayed close to Jesus until His death (Matt. 27:56).

There were other disciples, male and female. Mary of

Magdala, Joanna, Susanna and others followed Him and helped tend to the needs of the group around Him. Some of His disciples, no doubt, contributed to His living so that He could minister without having to work at His trade.[56]

Others like Philip, Nathanael, and Matthew came along to follow Him. Thomas, Thaddeus, Simon Zelotes, and Judas (who would betray Him) all followed Him. Jesus' earthly family was generally slow to follow Him. Yet James and Jude, His cousins by Mary Cleophas, and Mary herself later joined Him. At the cross we see His mother beside Him.

In this larger group of formal and informal followers emerged an inner circle. James and John seem to have been close to Jesus as well as John and Peter. The twelve who eventually are named as permanent followers of Jesus became the "apostles" who would spread the Gospel into Jerusalem, Judea, Samaria and unto the uttermost parts of the earth. Yet, none of them were theologians. None were prophets. They were instead ordinary persons who were commissioned by their Lord to evangelize all who would come into contact with them. No hierarchy existed among them. They called themselves brothers and shared in the evangelistic commission together.

From the very start the disciples caught Jesus' method of winning people to Him. Jesus pointedly said to the first disciples He called, "Follow Me." That is precisely what it would take to belong to Him—a life-style that followed Him.

When Philip, for example, was commanded to follow Jesus he was stirred to action. He repeated the pattern. He found Nathanael. Each one would win one. That's evangelism. And that was the way Jesus built His band of followers. The normal work of the kingdom of God can be seen in this pattern.

Jesus trained His followers using one of His favorite word plays. He made them "fishers of men." The disciples did not

understand all that Jesus taught. Even to the end, they were
confused and bewildered with the events that unfolded. But
Jesus devoted Himself to their training. He spent time with
them talking to them along the way. He warned them against
the cares of the world, the Pharisees, and false teachers. He
demonstrated His love for them and others time and time
again. He corrected them when they bickered among themselves. But He taught them patiently and carefully all the way
to Jerusalem where He demonstrated His greatest love for
them and the world on the cross. Perhaps the greatest summary of the way He wanted them to evangelize can be found
in John 20:21, "As the Father has sent me, even so, you I
send." Jesus intended for the disciples to imitate His life with
everyone they met just as He had demonstrated the Father to
them. He had shown the Father to all kinds of people. The
disciples were to do the same.

Christ spent large amounts of time with needy unbelievers.
He did not speak at them in terms of preaching at them.
Rather He cared for them. He ate and drank with them. For
example, as Matthew Prince explains, immediately after
Christ's call of the four, Peter, Andrew, James, and John,
Christ met a leper. "Christ touched him and freed him from
the hopeless misery of his disease. Christ then made himself
available to people in a home."[57]

Prince goes on to illustrate Jesus' contact with ordinary
people by saying that Jesus made 132 recorded contacts with
people as He taught, discipled, worked with individuals and
groups, healed, encouraged, warned and ministered to people's needs. "Ten of these [contacts] were in the temple and in
synagogues. The other 122 were with people where they
lived."[58]

Jesus spent most of His time being available to people.
Marketplace evangelism operates on the premise that we as

Christians should spend as much time as we possibly can with those who need Christ; in the workplace, at play, in social clubs, in hospitals, at school—wherever people are. If we follow Christ's example, we will break out of the "holy huddle" where the only people we know are already Christians.[59] We will become salt and light in a lost world.

The Church He Founded

On the day Jesus departed into heaven, He left them a promise. It contained three significant points:

1. They would receive *power* from on high.
2. They would become *witnesses* for life.
3. Their influence would reach *the whole world*.

No doubt they did not understand the implications of Jesus' promise at first. But when Pentecost dawned they began to envision that something extraordinary had happened to them. Suddenly, they were bold about their faith. Days before they had hidden in terror. Now they faced with new assurance the same people who had killed Jesus.

They watched people repent and confess Jesus by the thousands. They saw the Gospel expand to the Gentiles. They saw their tiny band of believers grow to the extent that seven men had to be appointed to wait tables just to take care of the physical needs of the many hungry, searching people that came to Jerusalem's church. They continued together, breaking bread, praising, praying, and learning together from the apostles.

How difficult was it for the early apostles to evangelize? Perhaps a better question might be, what advantages and disadvantages did they encounter as they witnessed? Obviously, one significant advantage that has been mentioned earlier in this book was the ease of communication. The Romans had seen to that. As Michael Green has explained, un-

der the Roman Empire you could go from the Black Sea to
the Bay of Biscay without fear of being robbed.[60] The Roman
roads made long journeys more possible. The language was
common. Greek was spoken in all the major cities. Their
faith was novel. No one had heard the gospel before, so their
message created interest.

One problem today is that so many people have "over-
heard" the gospel that they have not really heard at all.[61]
That is, they have never let it soak into their lives. They have
just become familiar with the gospel but it has made no real
impact on their lives. This was not so in the early days of the
faith.

But it was difficult for the early believers to witness also.
These men were not men of stature. They had no political
power. They had no learning. They had no structure to support them or any denomination to lean on for resources.
But worst of all they grew to be hated by both Jews and Gentiles alike. Race separated them. Class separated them.
Society was not interested in reform and religion. And yet,
with these obstacles, they succeeded beyond their wildest
imagination.

How did they succeed? What made their evangelism so
special? Again, Michael Green explains that they were new
people.[62] They were converted. They had died to their old way
of life and were alive in Christ. Perhaps today the reason why
evangelism is so difficult is that so many in the church have
passed by new life in Christ but have never let it possess
them.

These early Christians were completely dedicated to their
task. They were willing to leave family, friends, security, and
even give their lives to tell others about Jesus. They had a
sense of joy that was contagious. They sang in prison. They
prayed and praised God while being tortured and killed.

Their love for one another astounded others. They shared all things and none counted anything as his own. They were a people who lived against the backdrop of the resurrection and looked forward to the soon return of their Lord.

Paul and Evangelism

Paul is one of the best examples of the evangelist in the marketplace. Can you envision Paul, at work making tents during the day to support himself, talking to clients who wished to buy his tents, talking to fellow workers in the marketplace, and then teaching small groups of people in the evenings? Certainly Paul is a model of what the early church tried to get everyone to do. How have we missed that model today?

If we look deeper into the life of Paul, we can see how he related to others in his ministry to them. Questions might arise. How did Paul establish churches? How did he choose those he would leave in charge of the churches? And, how did he choose to do evangelism among the people of his day?

How Paul Established Churches

It is probably safe to say that Paul saw himself possessed of a message he had to share. His basic philosophy seemed to be like that of a "Johnny Appleseed"—instead of appletrees, he planted Christ in the hearts of groups of people he met. He would go into a city, possibly trade in the marketplace, and go to the Synagogue where he would seek those people who seemed to be looking for answers to God.

One such occasion is mentioned in Acts 13. Paul went to the Synagogue in Antioch of Pisidia. On the sabbath Paul and his friends went into the synagogue and sat down to listen. After the reading of the law and the prophets, the rulers of the synagogue asked Paul and his friends to comment on

what they had read. Paul stood up and began to share his
faith with them.

Paul began by confirming their faith. He traced their faith
through the ages and culminated with the story of Christ.
The people begged Paul to come back next sabbath to tell
them more. No doubt during the week Paul and his friends
kept up the dialogue. In fact, by the time the next sabbath
arrived, the whole town seemed to have turned out to hear
more of Paul. It upset the religious leadership of the city so
much that they tried to discredit Paul. Paul traveled to the
next town and repeated the whole scene again.

In each city it appears that a small group of believers gathered to form the nucleus of a church. Paul spent his time visiting in homes (Acts 20:18) and teaching publicly, always
encouraging believers. Paul and Barnabas visited these believers in every city where they had proclaimed the gospel
and where people had believed. No doubt they taught them
and ignited within them a desire to reach out to others and to
imitate the life of Paul and Barnabas with regard to evangelism.

The early Christians immersed themselves in the study of
the gospel as Paul proclaimed it. They knew the story backward and forward. They applied it to their lives and showed
others how the gospel answered their deepest questions.

> They knew the good news was like a sea: a child could pad-
> dle in its shallows, but a giraffe would be out of its depth
> before long. No five-minute sermonette and challenge for
> them! Paul could argue all day with the Jewish leaders [see
> Acts 28:23]. He could talk til Eutychus fell asleep and out of
> the window—then, after the interpretation, resume til dawn
> [Acts 20:7-11]. He could hire the lecture hall of Tyrannus
> during the hot dead hours in the middle of the day and fill it
> with eager enquirers [Acts 19:9]. If it required, Paul would

stay two years in a place like Ephesus in order to convince people about Christ.[63]

For Paul, finding believers to talk to was a simple matter. He just cut to the heart of people's searching and called them into accountability with the gospel. He talked to the polytheist at Athens, to the common citizens in Antioch, and to a jailer in Philippi. Paul and the early believers told others of a person whose life held the answer to all the searching and restlessness that the common people endured. Paul knew the religious leaders of his day would never admit their need for Christ. They were too busy keeping their religious establishment intact. But the average man or woman in the marketplace had needs to be answered. Paul and the early church moved their gospel into the marketplace where these needs could be met. That is the challenge of the church today. It must move out into today's marketplace where the same kinds of needs exist that were evident in Paul's day.

How Paul Chose Others

Paul chose others to help him. Each time, it appears he chose people to surround him that had the same kind of evangelistic fervor he maintained in his life. He chose Barnabas, Silas, Timothy, John Mark, Erastus, Aquila and Priscilla, to name a few.

These friends of Paul were laymen, not trained preachers. Barnabas owned land. He was probably a well-to-do businessman (Acts 4:36), yet Acts seems to say that Barnabas preached and taught just as Paul did (Acts 11:25-26; 13:43,46). Aquilla and Priscilla worked at the same trade as Paul but they argued (or taught) in the synagogue alongside Paul every Sabbath (Acts 18:1-4). Timothy was a young man, well spoken of, whom Paul felt he could train to follow in his footsteps. Erastus was called Paul's helper. No doubt

Paul discipled these people and filled them with the same fervor he had.

Surely, it can be that way today. I can remember certain laypersons who greatly influenced my life.[64] These have been people who imparted their gifts to my life on behalf of Christ. I learned from what they had to say to me. They taught me the value of demonstrating my commitment to Christ before others. I learned what life-style witnessing was from my barber.

My barber always had his Bible laid out on a table in his shop. He kept his radio tuned to a radio station that played Christian music. If you climbed into his barber chair you were bound to hear a gospel song or a message from a preacher. He displayed gospel tracts near the door and I saw people picking them up often. His shop was given to Christ. His clientele had no doubt about his faith. He often witnessed to me as a young boy. I can remember that he would speak quietly to me as he cut my hair about how Christ had changed his life and how He wanted to change my life. He was a great influence in my coming to Christ.

Today, there are thousands of Christian laypersons who work in the marketplace. They are barbers, doctors, construction people, nurses, waitresses, and so on. Each has a sphere of influence. Like the early church they need to "gossip about Jesus" in their marketplace, wherever they go, like my barber used to everytime I sat in his chair.

What better example could a Christian businessman or woman set than to seek to have every employee under his or her care know about Jesus. I have a friend who operates a small business. Every week, he gathers all his employees together for prayer. Some of them are lost but he prays for their needs. I know of doctors who quietly witness to their patients. The manager of a large grocery store chain in our city demonstrates his faith to every one of his employees by offering them counseling and direction when they have problems. Paul was aggressive in his faith. People today are not so much turned off by the gospel but by shy and lackluster witnesses. When the average person can see our faith in action in the marketplace, they will want what we have because they will know that our faith is not just for the church house but for every day.

The Foundation for Evangelism in the Early Church

The early church was a success in terms of its evangelistic outreach. There are several reasons why. First, they were devoted to one another. Jesus had taught them the model of love that sought the highest for others. He had demonstrated that kind of love time and time again, until they caught it. Hence, the early church cared about those who came into this midst after Pentecost. They learned to encourage one another. They sought to meet one another's needs and they took every opportunity to preach the gospel wherever they could.

Their fellowship was solid. It was so important that the seven were chosen from among them in order to keep any problems of fellowship from getting out of hand. They also kept their priorities in order. They knew that preaching the gospel, or telling the gospel, was more important than anything. So the appointment of the seven was one way to handle the need at hand and give time for the continuation of evangelistic outreach. They refused to be detracted from their primary goal.

The early church had a dynamic worship that centered on the Lord. The church at Antioch was characterized as one that fasted and prayed. They taught one another about Christ and they shared in their leadership responsibilities.

But most of all the early church looked beyond itself. It was not easy. Peter had to be shown in a vision that the gospel was for Gentiles as well as Jews. He had to participate in the coming of the Holy Spirit to the household of Cornelius. He was amazed that the Holy Spirit had transcended race and culture. Later, under the ministry of Paul the early church would expand throughout the whole Empire and be made up of Jew and Gentile alike.

In spite of all its struggles and obstacles the early church kept its eyes on Jesus. They had a passion to tell others about Him. And that passion translated into an evangelistic fervor that could not be contained.

Paul did evangelism in much the same way that it was done by others in the early church. Again, Michael Green has identified correctly the pattern that can be seen.[65] Barnabas was so gripped by the gospel that this landowner sold his land, gave his money to the church and became, like Paul, a slave to Christ. He encouraged everyone in his path . . . people like Paul, and became known as the son of encouragement. How we need more laypersons today who will encourage others in their faith.

Philip, from Caesarea, took the challenge of sharing his faith seriously. He witnessed to everything that moved. His business background had probably caused him to come into contact with all kinds of people. Since he had done business with all kinds of people it was not unusual for him to witness to all kinds: Samaritans, Ethiopians, and the like. He even kept an open house. People must have gone in and out. He not only had the gift of evangelism but also of hospitality. Other examples abound of how the New Testament characters told their story as they did business, as they traveled, and as they entertained people in their homes. No doubt they were a people on mission.

What Should the Church Be Today?

The church of today should be every bit as evangelistic as the early church in terms of its zeal for souls. Unfortunately, churches today have become so structured and programmed that they often exist under the power of their own bureaucracies rather than under the power and influence of the Risen Christ.

Even our denominations today have become an end unto themselves. We push programs and segment the gospel to the degree that our trust often lies in our programs, slogans, themes, our giant budgets, church and denominational staffs, and our creativity rather than in the personal presence of Christ with us.

The church today must interact with the world, community by community. For any church to exist apathetically alongside a lost community is a denial of the power of the New Testament church. As long as one is lost in the community, the church must be aggressively in pursuit of that lost person. There is always a tension between the lost world and the church. That tension lies in the calling of people to accountability with the Risen Christ. That accountability is also seen in the church's ministry to the world. A church that fails to minister to its community is a contradiction to the pattern of the early church. Unfortunately, we have become segmented in our thinking. We separate evangelism, ministry, and mission in the church. Michael Green has noted, "The Christian world has been rather polarised between two extremes. One stresses the importance of preaching the gospel to all and sundry. The other stresses the importance of the cup of cold water in the name of Christ. Social and spiritual gospels are not alternatives: they belong together."[66]

The early church was not so guilty. It was aflame with evangelism and ministry. The New Testament picture of the Jerusalem church is that it was reaching people for salvation and feeding them and taking care of them all along. Churches today need that vision.

A church today might describe itself as a ministering church. Another, an evangelistic church. Or still another as a mission-minded church. In the spirit of Paul, is the gospel divided? Is Christ divided? Certainly not. A New Testament church is always a mission minded, ministering, evangelistic church. Like a three-legged stool, it takes all three to keep things in balance. Without one or the other, things fall apart.

The church of today must be a catalyst in the marketplace. It must empower each person with the desire to reach the lost around them, to minister to them and to engage them in the mission of the church. It must be a fellowship filled with love, praise, power, and devotion to Christ. It must be single-minded and have one passion—Jesus. Otherwise, it stands unfaithful to the church Christ established and died for.

3
The Good Old Days

It is commonplace to say, "Evangelism is not what it used to be." It is correct to say, "It never was." One of the disgusting things about getting old, having escaped total senile dementia, is having to hear so many misrepresentations of what has happened in your own lifetime. Add to that nausea the knowledge that once a misstatement or misinterpretation makes the printed page or microfilm, it becomes "sacred" history.

Nonetheless, it would be difficult to overestimate the value of historical study. That being true, the challenge is for impartiality in researching and reporting. It is not surprising that the noted church historian, A. H. Newman, wrote,

> As the aim of the church historian should be to ascertain and to represent the exact facts in their relation to each other and to the times and circumstances concerned in each case, it is manifestly desirable that in the process of investigation he should deal as impartially with his materials as does the chemist with his specimens.[67]

Certainly our goal should be as precise in the more specific history of evangelism. Sympathy with evangelism historians is heightened, however, if you have ever tried to get accurate reports from last week's revival meetings.

Our objective in this study is a very abbreviated look at evangelism by all the people of God through all the centu-

ries. To get a wide-angle picture is difficult because evangelism reporting usually focuses on leaders; whether apostolic,
Constantinian, early American, or contemporary. However,
just as Augustine gave credit to his mother for her prayers
and influence in his conversion, most people in their testimonies today speak of more informal and nonprofessional influences in helping them become Christians. So much of the
evangelism ministry of ordinary, everyday Christians will be
read between the lines. Michael Green's appraisal is appropriate: "The very fact that we are so imperfectly aware of how
evangelism was carried out and by whom, should make us
sensitive to the possibility that the little man, the unknown,
ordinary man, the man who left no literary remains was the
prime agent in mission." Green quoted Harnack, "It is impossible to see in any one class of people inside the church chief
agents of the Christian propaganda."[68]

Evangelism Before Constantine

Latourette divides the pre-Constantine period into three
subperiods: 1. The Apostolic Age; 2. From the latter part of
the first century after Christ to the close of the second century; and 3. From the death of Emperor Marcus Aurelius to
Constantine. We discussed the first period under the New
Testament period. Even less information is available in the
second period. Newman reports that by the end of the Apostolic period the gospel had spread throughout Asia Minor,
Greece, Italy, and possibly even further west.[69] While we have
evidence that Christianity continued to expand during this
period we have little information about the methods and approaches. We do know that as Jewish influence waned the
Hellenistic (Greek) influence and atmosphere prevailed. The
expansion of the new movement geographically followed
the main trade routes to the cities and areas touched by Hel-

lenism. Because of Hellenism, the Christian Movement had cultural and political advantages, but also they had the disadvantage of being one of many new religious movements coming out of the ancient East to the populous cities.[70]

Along with growth of the Christian movement and its impact upon the lives of many people there was also some corruption and contamination coming by osmosis from the very influences that helped them spread. Pollution from the outside world perhaps was a greater handicap than the ever-present persecution.

Persecution

Persecution persisted during the period because the Christians were persistent in their proselytism. By its very nature the Christian religion must be universalistic in its outreach. All are lost from God, God desires to save all, and all who hear and believe will be saved. It is as simple as that. The Romans tried to be tolerant, but because of their own superstitious beliefs they were afraid for their subjects to refuse to worship the gods, who they thought protected them from enemies and guaranteed success and prosperity. The Christians could not tolerate any kind of recognition of the gods; therefore they lived dangerously.

From the perspective of the end days of the twentieth century it seems rather strange that civilized governmental leaders would allow violent religious persecution. It would not surprise us that political leaders would use religion as a tool to promote themselves, or as a pawn to protect themselves. On second thought, could the difference in the Roman Empire then and the Western world today be more in procedure than practice?

Most of the emperors of the Roman Empire during the second and third centuries did not so much practice persecution

as they permitted it. In some cases they simply forbade proselytizing, which to most Christians was very serious persecution. There were laws against unauthorized religions because
of the superstitious belief that there was an agreement between Jupiter and the empire that if the subjects of the empire worshiped the gods the empire would be protected from
its enemies and the country would be productive. Whether
they believed it or not the emperors were politicians and there
was usually someone to complain. So persecution was a
problem from Trajan (98-170) to Diocletian (284-316). One
of many paradoxes is illustrated by the fact that Diocletian's
wife, Prisca, and his daughter, Valeria, were said to be Christians.[71]

In addition to the intolerable relations between the followers of Christ and the state they had no sympathy from
the influential society of their day. Not only were Christians
mostly poorer people, but regardless of class and culture they
could not be popular because they refused to participate in
sins of the popular classes among the Romans. Christian enthusiasm was also like a rasp to the sensibilities of the philo-
sophical people of the day. Christians not only, therefore,
made their natural enemies, but found themselves devoid of
natural friends.

Why Christianity Spread Before Constantine

Despite all the disadvantages and discouragements, the
Christian movement spread. Believing they were being led by
the Spirit of God these followers of the Way often demonstrated their optimistic dedication. Obviously the environ-
ment effected the spread of the gospel, but did not control it.
Political, cultural, religious, and economic conditions were
faced daily, just as the farmer faced weather conditions daily.
In both situations there are temporary adjustments, but the

preparation of the soil, the sowing, cultivating, and reaping seasons go on.

A. H. Newman lists the methods of Christian "propagandism" in process during this period:

> The primitive Christians were essentially missionary. Each believer regarded it as incumbent on himself personally to propagate the faith that had saved him. Christians worked:
>
> 1. Privately, among friends and relations, by whom, however, they were often cast off as a result of their becoming Christians.
> 2. In the Oriental cities and villages the custom of talking at the corner of the streets prevailed to a great extent. An earnest Christian would thus frequently find opportunity to draw together a knot of hearers and to tell them of Christ.
> 3. Artisans of various sorts often found opportunity to spread the gospel among their fellow workmen.
> 4. After the time of the Apostle Paul, most of the spread of the gospel was effected, not by direct missionary efforts, but by the moving hither and thither throughout the empire of artisans and tradesmen, who planted Christianity wherever they went. So also Christianity was frequently spread by persecution, each fugitive forming a new center of Christian influence.
> 5. The burning enthusiasm of the early Christians was contagious. The minds of many were troubled. They could no longer believe in the decaying paganism which the philosophers had taught men to despise. Christianity, as represented by its enthusiastic devotees, met the felt needs of men. Its doctrine of the equality of all men before God, and the worth of all human souls, its promises of future happiness, such as would make present suffering of small consideration, tended to elevate them and deliver them from despair. The abounding charity of the early Christians, at a

time when poverty and distress abounded, drew to their fellowship multitudes of the depressed classes.

6. The Christians were obliged to labor for the most part secretly. They could not hold public services to which the unconverted could be invited. Their assemblies for worship were almost exclusively of church members. Only after one had been led to accept Christ did he gain access to the conventicles of the Christians. But the degree of secrecy necessary varied greatly at different times and at different places. While the Christians were on amicable terms with the Jews, whose religion was tolerated, they had more freedom. When they became objects of hatred to the Jews their freedom was less.

7. Attention has already been called to the hundreds of thousands, if not millions, of Gentiles who had come under the influence of Jewish life and thought throughout the Roman Empire. It is highly probable that a large majority of the converts of Paul and his associates were such; and it is certain that a still larger proportion of the converts of Judaizing Christian missionaries, outside of Palestine and Egypt, were Jewish proselytes.

8. No doubt the great truths of incarnation and redemption appealed powerfully to many who had been under the influence of the mystery religions and Egyptian and Oriental theosophy.[72]

Latourette, in a chapter called "Reasons for Ultimate Success",[73] points out the difficulty of documented evidence of how Christianity spread during the second and third centuries. He mentions the successors to the New Testament leadership of apostles, prophets, evangelists, and pastor-teachers. He calls attention to the fact that

the chief agents in the expansion of Christianity appear not to have been those who made it a profession or a major part of their occupation, but men and women who earned their livelihood in some purely secular manner and spoke of their faith to those whom they met in this natural fashion. Thus when Celsus denounces a religion which spreads through workers in wool and leather and fullers and uneducated persons who get hold of children privately and of ignorant women and teach them, Origen does not deny that this occurs. In the commerce and travel which were so marked a feature of the Roman Empire, the faith must have made many new contacts through Christian merchants and tradesmen.[74]

Constantine and Evangelism

From the point of view of New Testament definitions of evangelism, Constantine looks like a politician, and that is not to say that all politicians are bad. It is to say that coercion and manipulation are not evangelism. And New Testament Christians did not take too well toward people using it for their own personal gain (see Acts 5:1-10; 8:18-24). While we certainly cannot judge his conversion experience or his religious motives, church historians do not make him look good.[75] They not only report on his murderous political practices, but more than imply that his conversion was a convenience in overpowering his enemy, Maxentius.

Eusebius, an historian contemporary with Constantine, reported what Constantine told him personally about his conversion. He said that,

after noon, as he was praying, he had a vision of a cross of light in the heavens bearing the inscription "Conquer by this," and that this was confirmed by a dream in which God appeared to him with the same sign and commanded him to make a likeness of it and use it as a safeguard in all encounters with his enemies.

Eusebius reported that he saw the banner made in response to the vision and gave a description of it.[76]

Whatever one may say about the genuineness of his conversion, or his motives in practice, Constantine favored the Christian religion with every possible political advantage. No doubt some people, maybe many, came to know the Lord Jesus because of him. If so, praise God that He can use some mighty messy messengers and can serve the bread of life on some terribly dirty dishes. If a state can do worse by the Christian religion than to persecute it, it must be to make it the state religion. What appears to be growth in the church may sometimes be a swelling.

Early Evangelism

Notwithstanding all that can be said, and should be said, about the imperfections of a state church, and the abuse of power during this period and afterwards, it should be noted that some people, clergy and others, were devoted to evangelism. According to Latourette,

> A kind of mass conversion was in progress . . . Everywhere the actual work of conversion and the attendant instruction were carried on by the Church itself through many individual Christians.[77]

Some of the bishops did "the work of an evangelist" and lead their people in it. One such was Martin of Tours. Born to pagan parents, he followed his father into the military. It was during his hitch in the army that one cold day he divided his cloak with a beggar and the next night dreamed that he had seen Christ wearing the cloak he had given away. This seems to have led to his conversion, after which he resigned the army to give his life to the cause of Christ. He made an extended trip to win his parents and succeeded in reaching his mother. He became a bishop and was known for his evangelistic zeal.

Another was Ambrose of Milan, who was known to have won many pagans, his most notable convert being Augustine. Augustine did evangelism by writing, giving to the world his *City of God* and other famous writings. He was known as a personal witness in his diocese where he served as Bishop of Hippo. His influence upon Luther and other leaders through the centuries is immeasurable.

John Chrysostom, famous preacher and Bishop of Constantinople, sent out evangelists from among his people. He practiced evangelism, wrote evangelism, led evangelistic movements, and preached the virtues of a consistent Christian life. He wrote, "There would be no more heathen if we would be true Christians."[78]

To search the pages of church history is to experience the thrill of discovering evangelistic missionaries at every level of society, culture, and education. Some searching is required, however.

Early Christian Social Ministries

The best evidence of genuine evangelism is Christ living in the converted. Jesus prayed for that (see John 17:23); Paul wrote about it (see Rom. 8:10; Gal. 2:20; Col. 1:27); and the early Christians practiced it (see Acts 2:44*ff*; 4:36*f*). When Christ lives in the converted, the converted live like Christ. This kind of Christlikeness proved to be effective evangelism through the first five centuries of Christian history. Latourette wrote a worthy word at this point:

> An important means of attracting converts was the extensive humanitarian activity of the Church . . . Through the prosperity which followed recognition by the state it was able to do still more. It built and maintained hospitals, hospices for

strangers, and houses for orphans, widows, and the indi-
gent.

When, in the fourth and fifth centuries, so much of the
structure of society collapsed through internal decay and the
barbarian invasions, the eleomosynary functions of the
Church acquired growing importance. In many sections, no-
tably in the West, the Church remained the one stable institution, the only protector of the weak and the sole refuge of
the poor. This must have led to numerous conversions. We
know, for example, that the Church reared and instructed in
the Christian faith many children of pagans who had been
abandoned.[79]

This is evidence that the leadership of the churches were
"equipping the saints for ministry."

Early Evangelistic Literature

It would be difficult to overestimate the importance of literature to the spread of the gospel. A. H. Newman says that
the literature of the first three centuries "stands next to that of
the apostolic age not only in time but also in importance."[80]
He emphasizes its importance from the standpoint of a
source of information to us and calls to our attention the wide
variety and diversified forms of teachings of the times. One of
the most important conclusions he reaches is that its inferior-
ity to New Testament books confirms the belief that the original writings were "presided over by Divine Providence."

Should it surprise us that some of the most revered of ancient Christian writers expressed beliefs so vastly different
from what most of us would consider orthodox today? This in
no way diminishes the importance of our study of them, but
does testify of the value of every generation having its own
dedicated and trained scholarship burning the midnight oil in
Scripture study. Furthermore, we can praise our Lord, as we

have previously mentioned, that God can save the lost with less-than-perfect evangelists whether they be professionals or laypersons. Among those early writers we mention Clement of Rome, who was contemporary with some of the original apostles; Ignatius, who probably wrote at the turn of the first century; "The Shepherd of Hermas," during the first half of the second century; and during the same period the better known Polycarp and Justin Martyr. Still other familiar names in early Christian literature are Irenaeus, Tertullian, Cyprian, Clement of Alexandria, Origen, and Dionysius of Alexandria.

Most of the well-known writers we have named not only figured in the spread of the Christian message, but contributed to the controversies which cast their shadow over the centuries and in many ways hindered the progress of evangelism. Which particular religious party one subscribed to became more important to many than getting the gospel to unbelievers.

Writers, teachers, preachers, and theologians, more than evangelists per se, contributed to the rise and growth of papal power in the Church. There seems to be a pattern, if not a principle, that the stronger the hierarchy the weaker the participation of non-professional people.

Early Church Leaders and Evangelism

In the East theologians like Eusebius, Athanasius, Cyril of Alexandria, Chrysostom, and John of Damascus made some contribution to evangelism. Even more could be said about those in the West like Ambrose, Augustine, and some others. Most of our evangelism story by its very nature links up with the Western Church. It is not difficult to understand why evangelism, especially by ordinary Christians, in centuries gone by, is difficult to research. Some of the more obvious reasons might be listed as follows: (1) The length of time eliminates most oral history; (2) The scarcity of written history; (3) The natural tendency of historians to give more attention to church leadership, church politics, and church controversy, than to church expansion because contemporary writers did the same thing; (4) The continued unsurprising practice of giving reportorial priority to professional religion leaders rather than laypersons.

Evangelism During the Middle Ages

A cursory look at the close of the fifth century would perhaps leave the student surprised that Christianity survived the demise of the Roman Empire, they were so closely identified, particularly following the Constantinian period. Geographically speaking, the millennium following A.D. 500 did leave Christianity having surrendered as much territory as it had gained. It is possible that there were actually fewer Christians, nominally, in A.D. 1500 than A.D. 500. The records, however, mean very little either way in terms of true definitions of the Christian life. Baptisms by military and political movements perhaps made little difference except statistically. To discover what actually happened evangelistically during the period is at best educated guesswork. Kenneth Scott Latourette called Volume II of his *History of the Expansion of Christianity "The Thousand Years of Uncertainty."* Latourette did seem fairly certain as to the processes by which the Christian faith was propagated. He mentioned first that the movements were largely from "frontier to contiguous frontier."[81] This would strongly suggest that much of the basic evangelism was done by those we would classify as laypersons who made converts as they went about their daily lives.

The second explanation given is not surprising to modern students of evangelism: "the faith was propagated largely by the peoples most recently won to the faith." The historian also pointed out that the influence of the Papacy diminished as the distance from Rome increased. An interesting observation, however, is the fact that monks, though their origin was mainly for the purpose of personal meditation, became some of the most diligent evangelists of the organized Church. There did seem to be more Papal initiative in evangelism in England.

Honesty demands the admission that many of the so-called converts through these centuries had no choice. Since they were brought into the Church by force their genuineness would be discredited. The other much more interesting and encouraging side of the equation is the evidence that successful invaders into Christian countries often become the converts. Latourette told a curious tale about how non-Christian upon facing discouraging results in overrunning a town cast lots to ascertain whether or not their gods were with them. Upon receiving a negative answer they were advised to see whether Christ would assist them. Following their victory they returned home honoring Christ "by observing fasts and giving alms to the poor."[82] What's new?

On a more serious note Latourette wrote, "Many (pagans) appear to have been attracted by the more satisfying answers which Christianity gave to the haunting questions of the meaning of human life and the fate of man beyond the grave." He continued,

> Many of the records of the conversions and the missions of this period are contemporary documents, or only one generation removed from the events. As one reads them, he is impressed by the enthusiasm and the conviction with which the faith was propagated . . . An assurance of the truth of the religion which they professed, a zeal for the destruction of its rivals, and the desire to give its benefits to others seem to have constituted the driving power of the missions of the pe-

riod. In this appears to have been the major cause of the
spread of Christianity.[83]

Some evangelists, both clerical and lay types, must be
mentioned by name, as having evangelized during the period
under discussion. One of the most prominent who demands
to be heard about is Bernard of Clairvaux (1091-1165),
called "the missionary to the monks," preached to thousands
inside and outside the monasteries on salvation by grace
through faith. Peter Waldo (1179-1218) could be classified as
one of the outstanding equippers of laypersons as evangelists. The Waldensians went out two by two, as Jesus had sent
His disciples, to the streets and homes of people, teaching,
preaching, distributing written materials, and generally witnessing to people.

A better-known evangelist of the period was Francis of As-
sisi (1182-1226). One day while reading about Jesus sending
out the twelve, he answered the call to poverty, preaching,
and ministry. His disciples at times numbered into the hundred of thousands. His and his followers' ministry extended
to meet the needs of people whatever or wherever their
hurts. One Franciscan, Berthold von Regensburg, a popular
preacher and evangelist, compared to Whitefield as Francis
did to Wesley.

Dominicus of Spain (1170-1221) also established an order
similar to the Franciscans. One of whose well-known followers was Meister Eckhart, the Mystic. Another was the
praying evangelist, John Tauler (1300-1361).

John Wycliffe (1320-1384) was a professor at Oxford, well-
known Bible translator, and organizer and equipper of lay
ministers. These lay evangelists, called Lollards, were some
of the most courageous of the time.

Girolamo Savonarola (1452-1498), a Catholic evangelist

of unusual ability, had the courage to point out the absolute necessity of each person going to Christ for personal forgiveness, the futility of praying to Mary or the saints. Though burned at the stake, he served in preparing his world for the Reformation.[84]

Pre-Reformation Hindrances to Evangelism

In the early church evangelism seemed to be spontaneous. Whatever the experience or event it seemed to culminate in more people following the Lord (see Acts 2:40-43; 4:4; 6:7; 11:21,24). It is difficult to know how much of this took place as a result of personal witnessing and it is also difficult to know how much personal witnessing and mass evangelism grew out of a constant awareness of the command of Jesus, and how much of it was spontaneous enthusiasm growing out of their own joy in the Lord. At first hindrances did not seem to work. For example, persecution seemed to generate enthusiasm rather than hinder (see Acts 4:23-31; 8:4; 16:25-34). Obviously, hindrances did become real and devastating.

1. Hindrances Within the Church

The first and most pernicious hindrance to evangelism seems always to be among those who are supposed to be the evangelists. As always, the most realistic enemy of evangelism is apathy. There is, and always has been, a kind of pragmatic universalism. There never has been the problem of a large number of Christians leaders verbalizing their disbelief in the need for people to repent of their sins and receive the Lord, or the need for people to tell others about the Lord. It is that our actions disprove our stated beliefs. In that respect the last thousand years are not too different for the last ten years.

A second inside hindrance to evangelism had to be heresy. For example, Gnosticism came in a dozen colors and shapes. There were several kinds of Monarchian heresies. There was Montanism, Novationism, and the cousins of these under different names. Their teachings were not always all bad. Sometimes they were like the Donatists, who in their commitment to straighten out other heretics, themselves taught heresy.

Thirdly, and closely related to the heresies were the controversies which separated large bodies of Christians. Is it possible that the heresies and controversies actually grew out of the apathy and diobedience? Uncommitted Christians are not happy and always have to find a scapegoat.

Another confusing paradox is that some of the same people whose names we have listed as evangelism leaders in their time were the leaders of some of the heresies which seemed to erode the ministry of evangelism.

2. Other religions, primarily Judaism and Islam

Even though early Christians had been cradled in Judaism, the Jewish religion was the Christians' first serious foe. Fortunately, this was not that true all that long. Unfortunately, Islam, sprouting from some of the same roots, continued to be a rival. During more than one period Islam made more rapid gains than Christians.

3. The Crusades

How can followers of Jesus of Nazareth be involved in military campaigns against opposing forms of religion, and justify it on the grounds they have a holy cause? Without a doubt there were those whose motives were altogether political. In the case of the crusades they usually succeed in keeping the religious motive for conquest at the forefront. On the one hand the planners and aggressors were military and political leaders, enlisting the help of the popes. In other cases the popes enlisted the support of European princes to help with leadership, but provided promises of forgiveness from sin, liberation from debts, along with assurance to the crusaders that they were rescuing the saints from enemies in the holy land. Fervent preaching by some of the same people we have listed as effective and dedicated evangelists was used to enlist participation and support. Throughout Christian history otherwise good Christians have confused ambition, aggrandizement, and emotion with spiritual devotion.

4. The Inquisition

Evangelism fervor was demonstrated by the early church and has been throughout Christian history. To desire other people to become Christian is as normal to the Christian as worship, but when it begins to express itself in coercion, manipulation, pressure, and force it not only ceases to be evangelism, but ceases to be Christian. There have always been some who confused evangelism without absolute requirements of conformity to doctrine. In the same denomination the particular doctrines which preclude fellowship change from decade to decade. For example, when I began attending pastors' conferences and conventions in Baptist circles the big issues were the ordinances of the church, especially the Lord's Supper. Not only did the churches I grew up in practice "closed communion" from other denominations, but participation was closed to the local congregation of Baptists. If I returned to a church where I had formerly held membership I was not expected to participate. Well, there have been more serious extremes in Christian history.

In 1232, a tribunal organized by the pope, was placed in the hands of the Dominicans to enforce conformity. They had the power to arrest without stating the reason, to try without witnesses, and to use torture to extract confession. Civil authorities were required under threat of excommunication to enforce the Church's sentence, which was usually being burned at the stake or other equally horrible methods of death.[85] That is as far separated from evangelism as military invasion is from hunger relief.

The Protestant Reformation

A well-known colloquialism is "A little learnin' is a dang'us thing." That might be said of the importance of the Protestant Reformation to a study of evangelism. To cover this significant period of history sufficiently to find much evidence of New Testament evangelism would require far more space than the study allows. To make a brief statement is to be simplistic and misleading.

Martin Luther apparently desired to be called an evangelist and was likely sincere in the desire.[86] He was evidently at his evangelistic best when he was translating or teaching the Bible, because he spent most of his time and energy in what would be more incidental to evangelism. His doctrinal emphasis upon the authority of the Bible, the priesthood of the believer, and justification by faith, were certainly evangelistic doctrines.

Clearly, John Wesley and many others have been blessed in their ministry of the good news as a result of reading Luther. Every person who enjoys the privilege of witnessing to others owes something to Luther (1 Cor. 3:6-8).

The Protestant Reformation, like mountain springs, broke out in different places, spontaneously, and independent of each other. Two or three years after the beginning of Luther's work, Ulrich Zwingli of Switzerland began his reforming work, without any particular reference to Luther. He, like

Luther, was reared and educated in the Catholic Church and became a priest. In his effective and popular preaching, he went much further than Luther in his return to the New Testament and rejection of many Catholic beliefs and practices. He did retain infant baptism, but unlike Luther, declared that it had nothing to do with regeneration. His views did not spread as rapidly as Luther's and his followers were pretty well absorbed by Calvinism. He did make a strong local impact, not only because of his strong following, but because of the moral and political impact of his ministry.

Luther was twenty-four years old when John Calvin was born in France. As a young man he was arrested because of his Protestant sympathies. He escaped prison, and while wandering over Switzerland, was spending the night in Geneva and heard the evangelist Reformer, William Farel, and was convinced he should stay in Geneva and work as a Reformer. He was soon recognized as a leader and became influential politically and religiously in the city. His message emphasized the sovereignty of God, God's grace, and the government as theocracy. Personally and in preaching he was much more strict than Luther. His followers were much more evangelistic in the usual definition of the word than was Calvin. They not only absorbed the followers of Zwingli, but in the United States they eventually almost absorbed the Congregationalists.

The Anabaptists, in some ways successors to the Waldenses and Bohemian Brethren, went further than any of the other Reformers in a complete return to the Bible. They received their name, not only because they would not baptize infants, but when those who had been baptized as infants sought membership they required rebaptism. Of course the name soon came to represent all the groups with extreme and different views. While the Baptists of today in most areas of the world would claim some kinship to the Anabaptist, there were some called Anabaptists, with whom most Baptists of today would not identify.

The Anabaptists in England had their official beginning in 1611, though some claim to have been there earlier than the other reformers. There were certainly Anabaptists in Europe before 1611 and many of them were undergoing heavy persecution a century earlier, including the well-known Balthasar Hubmaier, who was burned at the stake by Austrian authorities in 1528. His wife was martyred by drowning. The Anabaptists were much more evangelistic than other Reformers, and were often persecuted by the other groups.

Much of the reform work was done for political as well as religious motives, and some for purely personal reasons, as in the case of Henry VIII of England. He abolished papal jurisdiction over England and established himself as head of the church in order to procure a divorce from his wife. As a result of the newly established Church of England and a series of incidents which seemed providential, the Bible was translated into the language of the people. Also Puritanism, a by-product of Calvinism, made an impact in England and in America.

Pietism and Evangelism

Piety is usually positive in connotation and refers to religious devotion and reference to God. *Pietism* often suggests affectation and exaggeration, maybe even hypocrisy and superficiality. Here we are referring to reform movements of the seventeenth and eighteenth centuries. The movement directly and indirectly affected evangelism. Genuine religious piety would normally express itself in reaching others with the Christian message. This was true with the best-known Pietistic Reformers.

William Perkins, an English Puritan, is credited with being the "Father of Pietism."[87] Better known leaders were Jean de Labadie (1610-1674) of France, Philip Jakob Spener (1635-1705), Alsatian theologian; August Hermann Francke, born 1663 in Lubeck, and Nicholas Ludwig Zinzendorf (1700-1760), scion of an ancient Austrian family.

Labadie, a Roman Catholic priest, began small group Bible studies, gave emphasis to meditation and prayer, followed the Calvinistic concept of personal holiness, all the while moving further from his Catholic heritage. He joined the Reformed Church in 1650 and became a pastor in Geneva where his ministry among students gained many disciples. His evangelistic ministry seemed to increase. His preaching to them was primarily repentance. His methods were special evangelistic meetings, seminars for preachers, and organized cooperative even simultaneous campaigns. "There could also be a planned, simultaneous impact of preaching at a specific time at various places, thus pinning down the world, as it were, and leaving it no time to catch its breath." Labadie's call to such cooperative, united preaching on repentance was "probably the first call to systematic evangelism, something that actually did come, only much later."[88]

Spener was one of Labadie's students at Geneva and was also influenced by the English Puritan writers. In 1670 he began small group studies in his home, then moved to the church building, where the Bible became the basic text of study. His life and ministry served catalytically in the Pietistic movement and indirectly in future evangelistic movements.

As pastor he insisted that lay people should be involved in the spiritual ministries of the church. He discredited a merely intellectual belief or acceptance of a dogma and taught that regeneration by the power of the Holy Spirit transforms the total person.[89]

Francke was a "spiritual grandson" of Spener, studied and taught in the University of Leipzig, became active in forming and leading a Bible club, which though bitterly opposed, became a positive influence at the University and throughout Germany. While Francke was teaching at Halle that University became the center of religious influence in Germany. He also began outstanding social ministries, especially to orphans. To minister most effectively to social need he founded a school of political science for training the gentry, nobility, and other outstanding sons and daughters.[90] He sought to enlist "kings, statesmen, teachers, leaders" for training and service, while he preached repentance and forgiveness of sin as an itinerant evangelist.

Francke's best-known student at Halle was Count Zinzendorf, who was reared by his pietist grandmother, the Baroness von Gersdorf; entered Halle at ten years old and devoted his life to personal piety, world evangelism, and Christian ministries.

Even as he studied law at the University of Wittenberg and then while filling a judicial position under the Saxon government Zinzendorf devoted himself to theological study and Christian work. About 1722 he purchased a huge estate from his grandmother in Upper Lusatia and began the settlement of hundreds of Bohemian Brethren. Here they founded Herrnhut (Lodge of the Lord). The organization of Herrnhut was like the Waldenses, Bohemian Brethren, and Moravian Anabaptists—especially dedicated to training and sending evangelists throughout the world. His personal dedication and evangelistic zeal, his organizational ability, like that of the Moravian Brethren continued to be used of the Spirit of God, even in the ministry of John Wesley.[91]

Evangelism in American History

There has been at times a prevailing notion that the planting of America was very similar to the Israelite's possession of the Promised Land, that the early settlers were all God's people, and that during the early years America was just what God wanted it to be. Actually there was a mixture of motives among the early settlers, but God was at work as He always is and there is a marvelous evangelism story to be told. As in all history, even church history, identifying the evangelism story is like trolling for shrimp; when you empty the net you still have a large separation job.

Roman Catholic Evangelism in Early America

First we will discuss the planting of Christianity in America by the Roman Catholics. We will discuss it in three phases: Spanish America,[92] Portuguese America,[93] and French America.[94]

The Spanish explorers were professing Christians and many of them had a sincere desire to see other people become Christians.

They endured hardship, privation, and personal pain in their desire to convert the Indians, teach them agriculture, and industry, as well as their culture. Their task was clearly easier because they had government support. There would obviously be some coercion, but there was no force in the cruder sense. The same government which supplied support also provided educational and cultural advantages. Of course all these were advantages as interpreted by the Spanish explorers. Notwithstanding the genuine sincerity of many evangelistic missionaries, the moral and spiritual level of Christianity, including some among the clergy, was not very high. Therefore, spiritual life among the native Americans was often shallow and short-lived.

While there were many similarities between the Spanish and Portuguese ministries of church planting, there were also differences. There were no great movements of converted Indians in Brazil because the conditions politically and culturally were different to what they were in Mexico and Peru, for example.[95] However, "tens of thousands of Indians and Negroes had been brought within the fold of the Church."[96]

In "French America" there was interesting and impressive evangelistic effort, marked by "heroism and devotion." In some ways the permanent impact of the early Catholic ministries in America are immeasurable. In vast areas of the United States and Canada the missionary ministry of French Catholicism still lives. The religious factor was more important, by comparison to the French Catholic, than to the English Protestants in the thirteen Colonies. "In French America the longing for religious liberty was not a factor in inducing immigration and the Christianity was entirely Roman Catholic."[97]

Since our purpose in this study is evangelism, and history is only a part of that, space limitations preclude a full discussion of the thrilling story of religion in the birthing of this nation. Roman Catholic missions covered a large geographical area, instituted more missions for Indians and blacks, and won more Christian commitments before 1800 than did the Protestants, yet their impact upon the future of Christianity in America and the world was not as significant.

Protestant Evangelism in Early America

Certainly by the end of the eighteenth century a different shape of Christianity, and even more different shape of evangelism had emerged. Biblical scholars can better decide whether the new shape differs more or less from New Testament Christianity than that of the post-apostolic or medieval periods. With these questions in mind we will now approach evangelistic work in early American history, as practiced outside the Catholic Church. Again we will be impressed by God's ability to accomplish so much despite human frailties. Still again, we will be encouraged and inspired by the deep evangelistic wisdom and work of so many.

One of the serious obstacles to gathering evangelistic history is the tendency for church historians to use the words *revival* and *evangelism* synonymously. There is a close relationship because a spiritual renewal or revival among the people of God usually results in greater dedication in getting the gospel to non-Christians. Likewise, concentrated evangelistic effort usually results in a spiritual renewal among those already Christians. Also, one may refer to a revival of evangelism. Precisely, revivalism is something experienced by those who already have life. Evangelism is what happens to non-Christians to help them receive the new life. Our assignment is the latter and right now our focus is upon early America.

One reason for a new flavor in American evangelism was the new American social condition. America was a society in motion. The immigrants were largely people voluntarily on the move. However, the natives were involuntarily uprooted. A mobile society is characteristically an individualistic society. A static society becomes institutionalized and traditional. Obviously, the evangelism of early America made its appeal to individuals. There were some mass movements among the Indians where large groups were "converted to Christianity," but like Constantinian Christianity, and some other less coercive examples, mass conversions have more to say for them quantitatively than qualitatively. "The Protestant churches in

America which have the largest membership today and are the most evenly distributed throughout the nation are those which stressed the personal in religion at a time when American society was dominantly individualistic."[98]

The New World spirit of individualism and rugged pioneerism was a fertile field for the new free spirit which had come directly and indirectly out of the Protestant Reformation. We mentioned earlier the Pietistic movement, which by the middle of the eighteenth century was losing momentum in Germany, but not before it had made an indelible impact on evangelism in America. Coming directly from Halle to New Jersey, Theodore J. Frelinghuysen brought the Pietistic and evangelistic zeal needed for the times.

Another Old World movement moved propitiously into the "new ground" American field to produce evangelistic fruit. A group of Presbyterian chaplains had served in a Scotland army of occupation in Ulster in 1642. Their evangelistic work resulted in new churches, new pastors, and a hundred thousand new members of Presbyterian churches in Ulster. The impact of these churches seeped into the Church of Ireland and many of their members became dissenters. One such dissenter was William Tennent, a priest who migrated to New York and was received as a pastor into the Presbyterian Church. Tennent was the founder of the famous "Log College" in Pennsylvania which impacted evangelism in America for generations.

The Impact of Evangelism on American Beginnings

We Americans, especially politicians and religious leaders, have a tendency to overindulge when we talk about our forebearers. We idealize and idolize far beyond what they would desire or deserve. Many early settlers from England and Europe certainly had evangelism motives in moving to the New World.

Many of the settlers had evangelism as their primary motive and many of their supporters did so because of evangelistic motives. When Lord De la Warr and the Virginia Council were about to set sail, Rev. William Crenshaw preached to them:

> Look not to the gaine, the wealth, the honor, but look at those high and better ends that concern the Kingdom of God. Remember thou art a General of Christian men, therefore, look principally to religion. You go to commend it to the heathen; then practice it yourself; make the name of Christ honorable, not hateful to them.[99]

Rev. Robert Hunt led a worship service as soon as the Colonists landed at Jamestown in 1607, using a piece of ship sail as a shelter. We recognize his preacherishness in the fact that in those rugged circumstances he improvised a pulpit between two trees. Hunt was succeeded by Rev. Alexander Whitaker, who baptized Pocahontas. There seems to be no question about the sincerity, motives, or dedication of Whitaker. A man of means, he suffered and served at great sacrifice for the cause of evangelism.

Virginia, however, did not continue to be so strongly influenced by spiritual incentives as Whitaker and some of the Church of England leaders had hoped. Monetary gain seems to have surfaced as the principal goal.[100] Efforts to enforce participation, of course, were ineffective. With some exceptions the clergy were morally and educationally superior to those who would come representing the dissenting groups later, but the later groups did more evangelism in Virginia.

In New England religious motives, including evangelism, were preeminent. The Pilgrims who settled at Plymouth in

1620 were seeking better conditions in which to worship and a desire to propagate the gospel. Along with those worthy goals they desired better conditions to make a living. They had already broken with the Church of England and knew about persecution. While their story is legendary, their own reporting was without the halo later given them.

In the Massachussetts Bay area the settlers were Puritans who desired to remain in the church but purify it of its "corruptions and disorders." They did prefer congregational government and, therefore, were more Separatists than they admitted.[101] They did not desire to defect as radically as Roger Williams, William Coddington, or Samuel Gorton, who founded Providence, Portsmouth, and Warwick respectively.

In Connecticut evangelism motives were not evident in the oldest colonies. The Congregationalists became the prevailing church. They, along with some Quakers, Baptists, and Lutherans, made some evangelism contribution. In Delaware Swedish Christians did some evangelism among the Indians. William Penn's conversion and leadership among the Quakers was a permanent influence in America.

Our tendency to honor, and even embellish, the past seems to be more normal than naughty. We more easily recall and recount to our children the better qualities of our ancestors. But we perhaps honor the early settlers more by facing the fact that evangelism among migrating people was likely more difficult for those sincerely dedicated to it in early American history than for us. For some of them the evangelization of the Indians, and later the blacks, along with the white settlers, was their consuming compassion. They experienced some immediate victories with all these groups, but it was perhaps as much challenge to them in their day and circumstances as the twenty-first century is for us.

Of the one hundred one colonists who came over in the *May-flower,* only a mere dozen constituted the membership of the first church. Scarcely a fifth of the Massachusetts Bay settlers who founded Boston, and the other settlements about the Bay, were even professing Christians.[102]

So few of the church members among the New England Puritans even claimed to have been converted that by 1662 the "Half-Way Covenant" was adopted to allow unconverted people to be baptized, but not to partake of the Lord's Supper.

Dr. W. L. Muncy[103] wrote that only five percent of the population were church members in 1700, but rose to 20 percent by 1775. Then during the war years it dropped again to five percent by 1790. So you see their evangelistic assignment was about as tough as ours. Though their world was greatly different from ours, it was as difficult to evangelize. We can learn from them. An awakening did come, but for evangelism it was a "vival" more than a "re-vival."

The Developing American Evangelism

In all this it is encouraging to know the evangelism rain clouds were gathering to bring moisture to the dry fields of America in the early 1720s. Even before that there had been "mercy drops" of Indian evangelism. It had been difficult, partly because of the wandering Indian population, and partly because, while the sincere Christians were trying to evangelize their fellow countrymen, their fellow settlers were trying to exploit them. Regrettably, that has been true with every period of Christian missions history. Happily, there were countless sincere efforts and some marvelous successes.

Roger Williams, the first Baptist pastor in Providence, worked personally and fervently with the Indians, but was disappointed with evangelistic results.

The earliest extensive evangelistic work with the Indians was done by the Mayhew family. In 1641 Thomas Mayhew and his son, also named Thomas, purchased the islands Martha's Vineyard and Nantucket. The younger Mayhew began to try to win the Indians there to Christ, and in 1651 reported 199 Christians. In 1657 the younger Mayhew was lost at sea on a trip to England. His father continued the work until his death in 1682. His grandson, John succeeded him, in turn to be succeeded by his son, Experience; and he by his son Zachariah until his death in 1806. By then large number of Indians were working in the mission.

Simultaneously with the Mayhew ministry, John Eliot began an evangelistic ministry with the Indians. He learned the language, won converts, finally began establishing churches, and then translated the Bible for them. By then numerous native Indian pastors were trained. In addition to evangelism the Indians were taught agriculture and other ministries. Sadly the Indian ministry was largely devastated by King Philip's War, an Indian outbreak against the whites. Eliot, however, kept working with them.

Quakers, Christian Swedish settlers, and Moravians had a successful ministry to the Indian. In 1742 Zinzendorf himself visited the Iroquois.

Now getting back to the rain clouds of evangelism in America, some of them gathered about the Pietistic movement in Europe. Theodore J. Frelinghuysen was a Pietist born in Germany but identified with the Dutch Reformed Church. He was twenty-nine when he came to America and began his ministry in the Raritan Valley in central New Jersey. His evangelism centered in his belief in the necessity of conversion. Finally, after much conflict some young people began to respond, then adults, including deacons and elders being converted. He then began to extend his evangelistic ministry.

What took place among the Dutch Churches in Colonial America was typical of the effect of revivalism among all the institutionalized religious bodies in which it gained a foothold. Though causing long and bitter controversy, the individualized emphasis in the Dutch Church saved it from complete extinction in Colonial America.[104]

The evangelistic emphasis among the Dutch served to inspire evangelism among the Presbyterians in New Jersey, New York, and Delaware. These Calvinists seemed to forget their logic as they became concerned about individuals who needed the Lord. Their kind of Calvinism doesn't seem to hinder evangelism.

This brings us to some more evangelism rain clouds, the Irish connection. William Tennent came to America from Ireland in 1716. He had been a priest in the Church of Ireland. Tennent explained his change to Presbyterianism on the grounds that the Episcopal Church was "conniving at the practice of Arminian [sic] doctrine inconsistent with the eternal purpose of God."[105] One cannot discuss evangelism in eighteenth century America without the Tennent factor. William Tennent began the "Log College" school for preachers at Neshaminy, Pennsylvania, where he was pastor. This little school was not only the training center for colonial evangelists, but from its roots sprang other schools throughout the country.

Tennent had four preacher sons: Gilbert, the better-known evangelist, William Jr., John, and Charles. Gilbert's ministry as an evangelist was greatly affected by the influence and encouragement of Frelinghuysen and George Whitefield. See how the rain clouds gathered. Gilbert Tennent was one of the most controversial and influential evangelists in Colonial America.

Coming under the influence of Log College were John

Rowland and brothers Samuel and John Blair, who operated a school like Log College. One of their students was John Rodgers who was the first Moderator of the General Assembly of the Presbyterian Church of America. Samuel Davies, taught by Samuel Blair, became a great evangelistic leader in Virginia and succeeded Jonathan Edwards as president of the College of New Jersey.

Two well-trained, wise, and capable evangelism leaders in Colonial America were the two Jonathans: Dickinson and Edwards. Dickinson, the acknowledged leader of the Presbyterians, was slow to respond to the revival movement, and when he did respond, was a moderating influence so far as excesses were concerned.

Even better known is Jonathan Edwards, often called the father of the Great Awakening. Succeeding his maternal grandfather Stoddard as pastor of the Congregational Church in Northhampton, a revival began in his church in 1734. Within a year above 300 people in Northhampton had professed faith in the Christ.[106]

Edwards began to move among other churches and the great New England revival was on. Because of his best-known sermon, "Sinners in the Hands of an Angry God," it is easy to be misled into an unfair judgment of his preaching. Until George Whitfield came into his ministry he was a manuscript preacher who usually read with his finger on the line. Actually throughout his twenty-three-year pastorate he was a quiet-spoken, teacher-preacher, respected as a philosopher and scholar. He did preach some effective hell-fire-and-damnation sermons, but he mostly demonstrated tender compassion and love. He combined intellectual power and emotional expression in respectable and effective evangelism.

John Wesley and George Whitfield

How does one write about John and Charles Wesley, and
George Whitefield with moderation and brevity? In my own
study I have often been inspired and motivated by just looking
on the bookshelf at the thin, worn old brown copy of Wesley's
Journal.[107] John often referred to himself as a "brand plucked
from the burning."[108] The story of the five-year-old, fifteenth
child of Samuel and Susannah Wesley being brought out the
window of the burning residence of the unpopular Epworth,
England, preacher is a story of the hand of God in history.

Perhaps if the Wesley brothers appeared in your church
next Sunday, Charles would get more applause for his songs
than John would get for his sermon, but the world would be
poorer without either.

In Oxford University they and their friends in the "Holy
Club" were called "Methodists." So another fun name became the honorable label of a worthy denomination which
for years helped to color the evangelism picture of American
history.

Likely no conversion story outside the New Testament has
been told more often than that of John Wesley. Again the rain
clouds of the Moravian Brethren may have appeared no
larger than "a little cloud . . . like a man's hand" (1 Kings
18:44, KJV) when Peter Bohler, the Moravian, helped John
Wesley become a Christian on May 24, 1738, according to
Wesley's *Journal.* He was already thirty-five years old and
had served as a missionary to the Indians in America.

George Whitefield was born eleven years after, and died
twenty-one years before John Wesley. They met in Oxford as
members of the Holy Club. Their backgrounds were vastly
different. Wesley was a product of an English rectory, while

Whitefield grew up in an innkeeper's house and became a bartender. They complemented and influenced each other for the good of all of us. Whitefield was a spell-binding preacher while Wesley was a workaholic and organizer.

Wesley was disciplined with a mixture of scholarship and mysticism, while Whitefield was explosive, ecstatic, and dynamic. Whitefield was more Calvinistic, believing in the elective grace of God and the security of the believer. Wesley was Arminian in rejecting the doctrine of predestination and insisting upon the necessity of continuing the holy life. In everyday application those differences melted and flowed as compassionate contributions to the evangelization of eighteen-century America.

Baptist Evangelism in America

Baptists benefitted more than they contributed to the Great Awakening. They made an immeasurable contribution to civil liberty, democracy, the doctrines of the priesthood of believers, and the baptism of believers only. Doctrinally, therefore, they made a greater contribution to the cause of evangelism in early America than by aggressive participation in evangelism and revivals.

Roger Williams, born about 1604 and educated at Cambridge, came to New England to escape persecution, and served for awhile at Plymouth as pastor. He demonstrated unusual interest in the Indians, learning their language, and trying to minister to them. He was banished from the Colony in 1635 because of his convictions about soul liberty, but soon established Rhode Island as a democracy and the Baptist Church at Providence.

John Clarke, who worked with Williams, founded the second Baptist church at Newport in 1641.

An evangelizing influence among Baptists was the organization of the Philadelphia Association in 1707. But the Baptists generally were nonaggressive and did not participate with Edwards, the Tennents, Whitefield, and others in the revivals, often refused to open their churches to the revivalists. Yet they received growth from the revivals because of their doctrines. Many of the evangelistic Congregationalists, for example, decided they could not keep a pure converted church without rejecting infant baptism. They became Baptists and were much stronger in outreach and evangelism than the regular Baptists with whom they affiliated.

During the Revolutionary period Baptists in the South had faster growth than in New England. They also made progress in their commitment to religious equality and separation of church and state. Both of these causes were important to evangelism in the future.

At the beginning of the eighteenth century American Baptists numbered about 100,000, had one educational institution, Rhode Island College (later Brown University), several associations, no state conventions, no Sunday Schools, no newspapers or magazines. They did participate in the great revivals of the last years of the century and the first years of the nineteenth century. They were predominantly poor, illiterate, and educated pastors were few. But they grew rapidly during the early part of the century, and by 1812 numbered 172,972.[109]

American Baptist interest in world evangelism gained some momentum with William Carey's going to Indian in 1793. Missionaries Adoniram Judson and Luther Rice were converted to Baptists views and Rice came back to America to gather support for their work in India. Small societies were organized in the churches to support them. A group of representatives from these churches met in Philadelphia in 1814 and organized the Triennial Baptist Convention.

Their interest in the propagation of the gospel intensified and soon state conventions were being formed throughout the country.

The new denomination grew rapidly, developing Sunday School work, denominational colleges and seminaries, as well as the publication of Baptist newspapers. All this progressive change resulted in increased opposition, especially among the uneducated. But more divisive issues were to arise later. Before the middle of the century Baptists of the North and South would begin to draw party lines. There were some differences in their preferences about organization in the missions and other work. The slavery issue, unfortunately, loomed larger than desire to work together in evangelism.

The Birth of Modern American Revivalism

So much of revival evangelism is an American phenomenon that it seems appropriate to focus there. As the eighteenth century came to a close it would have seemed in order to talk of the "good old days" of American evangelism.

In 1790, church membership had declined to where only five percent of the people were in the churches. Morality was low. Sin was rampant. The Great Awakening had made a great contribution but the war years were bad for evangelism. Dr. Roland Leavell wrote of the liquor traffic in America at the time and went on to say,

The marriage vow was disregarded, and homelife degenerated. Gambling, vice, and profanity held sway. Infidelity so gripped the schools that no college had a dozen students who would admit being Christians. The churches grew empty and impotent.[110]

However, the foundations did not crumble. Many Great Awakening values remained. The Methodist denomination had been born and Baptists multiplied. Some older denominations had seen what could happen in God's economy. Religious liberty had been decreed and the beginning of the nineteenth century was to be a time of revival.

The revival of this period apparently began with the praying of Baptists, Methodists, and Presbyterians. It then spread in all directions throughout America. Colleges became involved. There were Hamden-Sidney and Washington in Virginia and Jefferson in Pennsylvania. Yale became a leader in the revival movement with Timothy Dwight as president, and a revival leader personally. The scope of Yale's impact was nationwide. All these schools became training schools for revival leaders. The "Second Awakening" was on the way and made a lasting impact upon evangelism.

Two of the outstanding preachers of the period were Lyman Beecher and Nathaniel Taylor. An outstanding "lay" type of revival leader in the period was Asahel Nettleton. He was not a pastor, would not receive remumeration, and his speaking was direct, searching, and simple. To his public speaking he "added house-to-house visitation and personal conference, and his converts were always thoroughly schooled in the fundamental teaching of Christianity."[111]

The "Camp Meeting" was born during this period and was led at first mainly by the Presbyterians. James McGready was the leader of the famous Logan County, Kentucky, revival in July, 1800. People came from up to a hundred miles, mainly in wagons, and camped for days. Another well-known revival was the Cane Ridge Meeting in Bourbon County, Kentucky. Barton W. Stone, a Presbyterian preacher who became instrumental in forming what became the Disciples Movement, was a leader in that revival.

Though the Presbyterians were active in the first camp meetings, they were participated in by a wide cross section of

people and groups. Many Presbyterians and other pastors opposed the excesses of the meetings and refused to attend. The
people came together in wooded areas, cleared out the un-
derbrush, and camped in tents, wagons, and on the ground.
They would trim the lower limbs from small trees so that
when people were overcome emotionally with the "shakes"
they could hold on to the saplings to prevent falling to the
ground. Of course many people would be seen on the ground,
writhing in anguish as they confessed their sins.

Because of this kind of behavior outsiders would gather
around for entertainment. There were reports of excessive
drinking, gambling, and fights around the perimeters of the
camp meetings. For most of us to comprehend this phenomenon at all we must fix our imaginations upon the frontier.
Unfortunately, some of us can fix our memories enough to
require less imagination, especially for some of the perimeter
activity.

It is also very important to remember that, while much of
this behavior may seem more bizarre than blessed, not only
did some good and holy things come out of those meetings,
but they made a contribution to our country, to the kingdom
of God, and to our lives.

The differences and divisions, as always, resulted in the
birth of new groups. The Cumberland Presbyterians came
out of this period. This does not suggest any similarity between them and the camp meeting practices any more than
your typical First Methodist or First Baptist Church is similar
to some of their distant cousins of the frontier. The Cumberland Presbyterians were born mainly because the Presbyterians were growing so fast they could not produce
academically trained pastors fast enough to meet the demands of the churches. So they lowered the standards for
ordination, formed new Presbyteries, and kept growing.

Perhaps the primary difference between some of these

groups and many New Testament churches is that the latter perhaps did not worry about the ordination. They likely let "laymen" be "laymen" as they continued to make their living at some other job and also give their leadership to the churches. Remember that many of the frontier preachers also made their living in the workplace; the only difference was they were ordained. Many would ask what the ordination added.

Of course another effect of rapid church growth in this period was the dilution of extreme Calvinism. They didn't so much change their Confessions as they ignored them in favor of more aggressive outreach to the lost and needy.

Some Lutherans, German Reformed, and Episcopalians were involved in the revivals, but the great protagonists of frontier revivalism were the Baptists and Methodists. Writing of the period (1785-1812), Leavell says the Presbyterians multiplied by three, the Baptists by four, and the Methodist by five.[112]

The Methodist continued the camp meetings and were more successful than other groups. Bishop Asbury often referred to camp meetings in his Journal. However their practice was not a primary method of evangelism, just one method.

By the end of the 1820s Baptists had a network of voluntary groups of churches called Associations. They were organized for cooperation in missions and evangelism, but some of these meetings were held in the woods, like camp meetings. They were attended by thousands of people, unlike the practice of today using the same kind of network and name, but more often attended by leadership to plan programs and transact businesses.

Excesses seem to be practiced in all large evangelism movements, but in the first half of the nineteenth century sane evangelism prevailed. By 1860 church membership had climbed from 5 percent of the population in 1790 to 23 percent.

Personalities in American Revivalism

Charles Grandison Finney seems not to have been directly effected by the revival movements at the time of the beginning of his ministry. While there was slight similarity to the evangelism of Frelinghuysen, the Tennents, Whitfield, Wesley, and Edwards, Finney was more similar to those who followed him than those who preceded him.

Finney's personal salvation testimony would have sounded perfectly normal in the community where I grew up.[113] I have known people to agonize over their salvation for days just like Finney did. The big difference is that those I knew about made their agony a public experience, going to the "mourner's bench" day after day in the revival meeting, seeking salvation.

I have no idea how many times I have heard preachers boast of their lack of education and the ineffectiveness of the educated preachers they knew. Though he made some marvelous contributions to education, Finney was guilty of that kind of deluded talk. While educated in some ways, he lacked a liberal-arts education. In formal schooling he would be like a high school drop-out. However, before he studied law, he was a schoolteacher. (I recall knowing school teachers who had not finished high school.) His law study and his theological training were as apprentice to a lawyer and pastor respectively. That meant he might have been well prepared in some respects and conveniently ignorant in others. Unlike Moody, Finney used acceptable language. Like Moody, he used what he had to the glory of God and to the good of thousands of people. In many ways he is the father of the revival evangelist, as we know him today. He gave a strong emphasis to the necessity of the conversion experience and the importance of human participation in the spread of the good news.

Finney was, without question, fully committed to God. His character was flawless, his motives were pure, and his courage was dauntless. His preaching was simple, Scriptural, and sincere. Wherever he preached, large numbers of people responded to his invitation. All the great evangelistic crusade leaders since his time can thank him for many of their methods. The person who wrote the closing lines of Finney's memoirs had no idea how prophetic he was: ". . . other generations will reap benefits, without knowing the source whence they have sprung."[114]

Dwight L. Moody

Born in Northfield, Massachusetts, February 5, 1837, and born again in Boston, April 21, 1855, Dwight L. Moody discovered the real meaning of the new life in Chicago. His landlady, Mrs. Hubert Phillips, had responded to his desire for a place to serve by suggesting that he go to the Wells Street mission of First Baptist Church. When he went there and volunteered his services the superintendent likely had no idea that what he thought was a casual suggestion was all in the plan of God for a life and a historical movement. The superintendent told Moody to go out into the alleys and the streets and round up some boys for a class.

With his charming personality, his godly zeal, and his ability to enlist helpers, Moody's class moved from smaller to larger facilities until he was having over 600 attend Sunday School. Remarkably successful as a salesman and businessman he had ambitions to be a faithful servant of God and a millionaire. Full commitment of his life to the former gradually decimated his ambition toward the latter, but his business abilities were always used by this "layman" in one of the most remarkable evangelism ministries of the centuries. One of God's gifts to him, which he used effectively, was to enlist the financial support of wealthy businessmen to support his ministry.

God also blessed Moody's winsome ways in making it possible for him to get the attention and then the love of attractive and capable Emma Revell. Emma was the opposite to Moody in that while he was healthy, strong, extroverted, dominant, impulsive, and uneducated; she was educated, shy, prone to poor health, conservative and discriminating. She loved, supported and taught him through the years of their marriage. Paul, their son, was quoted as saying of his father, "To the day of his death, I believe, he never ceased to wonder at two things—the use that God had made of him despite his handicaps, and the miracle of having won the love of a woman he considered completely his superior."[115]

Moody seemed always to perceive of himself as a "lay" person, rather than as a clergyman. During the early years of his Sunday School and Y.M.C.A. ministry in Chicago he was the organization and promotion person and others did most of the public speaking. When he did speak in emergencies he was usually effective and appreciated, albeit with some early experience of heckling and mockery because of his language deficiency.

A great influence and turning point in Moody's life was his work in military camps during the Civil War. He worked closely with the Army and Navy in planning and organizing the total spiritual ministry to the military and participated personally by evangelizing and ministering in other ways.[116]

It would be difficult even to conjecture the direction of Moody's ministry apart from Ira David Sankey. Moody heard Sankey sing in a Y.M.C.A. meeting in Indianapolis and bluntly told him that he should join him in his ministry. They prayed about it together, although Sankey later explained he had no idea of leaving his business in Pennsylvania. He did. One seldom reads a page about one of these stalwarts without the other's name being mentioned. In fact, before they left the city of Indianapolis Moody surprised Sankey by arranging a street service in which the two sang and preached. The street crowds responded. All kinds of crowds did for years.

On Sunday evening, October 8, 1871, a Moody-Sankey meeting was cut short by the noises of what is still well-known as the Chicago Fire. It seemed the city was destroyed. Homes, businesses, and fifty churches and missions were destroyed, including Moody's meeting places. While in New York raising financial support to rebuild, his prayers for Holy Spirit power in his life were answered. In fact, some others had been praying for this experience before Moody discovered the need.[117]

From then on there was clear evidence that God's hand was on the ministry of this man everywhere he went. This work omits the larger thrilling story of Moody's ministry which is so well-covered in so many written works. His testimony is still very much alive and bearing fruit, not only in Great Britain and America, but around the world. He sought to be the man who committed his life completely to God, and truly found what God would do with it. Maybe the rest of the world found out more completely than he.

It is no reflection on the ministry of men like R. A. Torrey, J. Wilbur Chapman, the two "Gipsy" Smiths, Billy Sunday, Sam Jones and dozens of others to say they followed in the wake of Finney and Moody as leaders of Mass Evangelism Crusades.

Billy Graham

The best-known of all vocational evangelists of all time is Billy Graham. He has been heard by more people than any other such evangelist who ever lived. The media classifica-

tion of "televangelists" does not enter into this discussion because most of the well-known media preachers do not claim
or practice evangelism as their primary ministry in the sense
of Graham and the other above-named evangelists. The term
televangelism came into use to describe a special program of
the Radio and Television Commission of the SBC in the late
1950s. Billy Graham was a successful evangelist after the
tradition of Moody, Sunday, and the others even before he
became a media celebrity. Many people do televangelism just
as many people do evangelism who are not vocational evangelists. Billy Graham is an evangelist who does televangelism.

Billy Graham was converted in an area crusade in his
hometown of Charlotte, North Carolina. The revival was led
by Evangelist Mordecai Ham. In his youth he served briefly
as a pastor but clearly felt the leadership of the Spirit of God
into a ministry of "full-time evangelism." He "paid his dues,"
as they say, to gain recognition by religious denominations as
well as world leaders in politics, business, education, and society in general. This earned recognition included his own denomination of Southern Baptists. He made an independent
decision to become a Baptist just as his wife Ruth made a
decision to remain a Presbyterian, as she had been reared in
a Presbyterian missionary home in China.

Even after he began to receive world recognition as an
evangelist, he was not immediately received enthusiastically
in his own denomination. Southern Baptist evangelism leadership, then in the throes of trying to develop a program of
evangelism for the entire denomination, were a little defensive about giving exposure to "an independent evangelist who
was connected with Youth for Christ." They admired and respected him, as they did Youth for Christ, but simply doubted
the wisdom of putting Graham on major programs.

Then in 1956 he was asked to speak to the Southern Baptist Convention on Home Missions Night. He brought, as expected, a marvelous message and displayed, as always, a beautiful and humble spirit, filling the house to capacity. He was "on" from then on among Southern Baptists, and has been recognized as their best known and most influential leader.

Immediately following that first major message by Graham to the Southern Baptist Convention, the newly elected leader of evangelism in the Convention was visiting with his retired predecessor.

The saintly veteran was all ears about the Convention he had been unable to attend. He was especially anxious to know how Graham came off. When he was told how well it went and how much God seemed to have used it, that grand old man of evangelism, with tears in his eyes, expressed his regret that Graham had not been invited earlier. The younger leader explained that he felt that the timing was propitious for the Convention, for Graham, and for the kingdom of God.

Later Graham requested the privilege of attending the annual meeting of state directors of evangelism, along with the Home Mission Board evangelism leadership, because, explained Graham, "I want to know what plans are being made for evangelism by Southern Baptist leadership." For some years following, when evangelism leaders had their planning conferences at the Ridgecrest Conference Center, Ruth and Billy Graham would invite evangelism leaders and their wives to the Graham home for tea during the Sunday break time.

Evangelist Billy Graham has made the following contributions to Christian history in his own time: (1) He is the best-known Christian in the world. (2) He is the most positive influence for Christianity for more people in the world than any other person. (3) He consistently demonstrated an uncanny ability, (no doubt a gift from God) to turn any interview, press conference, or public appearance into an opportunity to present the gospel in an inoffensive manner. (4) He has legitimized evangelism in broader circles than any other person in the last half century. (5) He has made evangelism easier in all its forms throughout the world. (6) Graham combines deep spiritual perceptions, dignity, and cooperation for effective ecumenism. His is not the only kind of evangelism. He has consistently said that local church evangelism is the best kind. But God has used, and will use, the ministry of Billy Graham. Hundreds of lesser-known evangelists are used of God's Spirit every day. People respond to people.

Southern Baptist Evangelism

The Christian religion is characteristically evangelistic. Most Christian denominations emphasize evangelism as one of their major objectives. Most major denominations have an evangelism department or division with elected leaders. They have excellent and attractive printed materials, films, tapes, videos, charts, books, and magazines. They have suggested programs for churches and groups. They are well prepared and practical. If followed faithfully and prayerfully they are effective.

Testimonies and materials from all these denominational groups indicate that if the programs were implemented as well as they are prepared, far more people would be Christians and most congregations would be growing.

Southern Baptists are an example. Their elected evangelistic leaders would unanimously agree that the Southern Baptist evangelistic reputation is better than their record. They are characterized as "strong in evangelism." Their evangelism is said to be "one of their greatest strengths." In reality their baptismal ratio is about one baptism for every forty-two members. The stated objective of the Southern Baptist Convention is "the propagation of the gospel." The purpose is "to provide a general organization for Baptists in the United States and its territories for the promotion of Christian missionaries at home and abroad and any other objects such as Christian education, benevolent enterprises, and special services which may seem proper and advisable for the furtherance of the Kingdom of God.

In the Southern Baptist Convention charter, evangelism was given as a program to the Board of Domestic Missions. Later the name was changed to "Home Mission Board." From the beginning the Foreign Mission Board considered evangelism to be the major reason for their existence. The Southern Baptist Convention was organized in 1845, but it began to move toward a denominational structure for evangelism in 1904. Len Broughton, pastor of the Atlanta, Georgia, Tabernacle Baptist Church asked for a committee of twelve to be appointed to study evangelism needs and report back.

The committee consisted of Len Broughton, George W. Truett of Texas, W. W. Hamilton of Kentucky, W. M. Vines of Virginia and Andrew Jackson Spears of South Carolina. The committee reported to the Southern Baptist Convention in 1906 with the recommendation that the Home Mission Board establish the department of evangelism and supply a leader. Following a moving message by B. H. Carroll of Texas, the Home Mission Board Department of Evangelism was established and W. W. Hamilton, a Ph.D. graduate of Southern Seminary, was elected as superintendent.

The Home Mission Board was generous in assigning five associates (as many as the department had in 1955). However, it was stipulated that these early evangelists were to earn their salary through revival honorariums. The plan must have been successful, for by the third year Hamilton had eleven associates with self-sustaining financial requirements.

The denominational program consisted mainly of revival meetings with Home Mission Board staff as evangelists. Hamilton led in conducting several simultaneous revivals by enlisting churches on one side of the city (or association) for two weeks, then moving the preachers and singers to churches on the other half of the area for the next two weeks.

Some of the first such associational simultaneous campaigns were in St. Joseph, Missouri, Wilmington, North Carolina; and Atlanta, Georgia. In 1908, the department conducted an evangelism conference in Hot Springs, Arkansas, with E. C. Dargan, Lee R. Scarborough, and H. A. Porter as speakers.

Evangelism conferences would be conducted on Friday, Saturday, and Monday before the Southern Baptist Convention sessions began on Tuesday. Some subjects for discussion were: "How to Get Ready for Revival," "Drawing the Net," and "Caring for Young Converts." Hamilton's book *Bible Evangelism,* to which I still refer from time to time, was often taught as a resource in evangelism.

Hamilton, after successful leadership as first evangelism superintendent, resigned to return to a pastorate and was succeeded by Weston Bruner in 1910. Bruner had as many as twenty evangelists working with him. Their primary ministry continued to be revivals. In 1912, they began an evangelistic ministry among college students in mountain areas and among blacks.

In 1918, Hamilton returned to the position with added responsibilities in raising money, encouraging churches to increase pastor's salaries, and helping them with church budgets. In 1922, O. E. Bryan came to the position as superintendent of evangelism and enlistment. Almost immediately Bryan resigned to head the "75 Million Campaign" to raise money to pay off Southern Baptist debts. One of the most significant contributions of the 75 Million Campaign was that it proved the value of a unified program of financing denominational ministries. Thus, the Cooperative Program was born in 1925.

In 1924 Bryan returned to the Home Mission Board, but only for a few months. He went to Tennessee to become executive secretary of the State Convention. You see, even with the rapid turnover they were electing capable people to the evangelism leadership. Hamilton went on to be president of Baptist Bible Institute, which was to become New Orleans Baptist Theological Seminary. But hold on, there are more seminary connections to cover.

Ellis A. Fuller was elected superintendent in October, 1925. He led in statewide simultaneous campaigns. Fuller worked closely with pastors, was dynamic and energetic, and took seriously his assignment. Once when Leonard Sanderson was in revival with the late Dr. Louie D. Newton, Newton told how tired and stressed Fuller had become under the pressures.[118] Newton sat him down and gave him quite a lecture about the need for relaxation and discipline in his personal life. He tried to convince Fuller that he couldn't get the gospel to everybody in a brief time and that he couldn't at all if he went down under the pressure.

Fuller resigned October 1, 1928, to become pastor of First Baptist Church, Atlanta. He went on later to be the dynamic president of Southern Seminary in Louisville. With the depression years, and the lack of financial support, evangelism leadership suffered. There was no leadership until 1936 when Roland D. Leavell was elected at the St. Louis Convention. The people cheered in jubilance.

Leavell was experienced in Baptist life, suave and dignified as a leader. He and J. B. Lawrence, executive secretary of the Home Mission Board, called on the Sunday School Board for cooperation in evangelism. The Sunday School was more and more recognized potentially as an evangelizing force in the churches. A "Standard Sunday School" had to be evangelistic, according to Arthur Flake, a recognized leader whose evangelistic leadership still lives. The Training Union was already giving leadership to "Disciple Training" in soul-winning. While Leavell was a revival preacher he gave great dignity and legitimacy to evangelism. He wrote some excellent study books and other materials, but he resigned April 1, 1942, to go back into the pastorate. He then went on to give great leadership for years as president of New Orleans Seminary.

Fred Eastman, pastor, First Baptist Church, Wichita Falls, Texas, was elected superintendent December 15, 1944, and served, despite some health problems, until October, 1946. To celebrate the Convention's 100th anniversary it was decided to promote simultaneous revivals in churches throughout the convention in 1945. M. E. Dodd, pastor of First Baptist Church, Shreveport, Louisiana, and world-renowned evangelism leader, was asked to work with Eastman in giving leadership.

Dodd succeeded in giving Southern Baptists a vision of the potential impact of most evangelism movements in simultaneous revivals. This was my (Sanderson's) first experience in simultaneous evangelistic campaigns. I worked in one in Dyer Association, Tennessee, which Dodd directed personally.[119] He had pioneered in radio evangelism and used it in the Dyer campaign. He also spoke at noon each day to a pastor/evangelist luncheon.

The 1945 event, the first national Southern Baptist simultaneous effort, was the catalyst for all such future campaigns for Southern Baptists. Eastman resigned October 1, 1946, and C. E. Matthews, evangelism director for Texas, was elected. Matthews had already been praying about the position. When J. B. Lawrence, executive secretary of the Home Mission Board, called Matthews, Matthews answered, "I know what you are calling about and the answer is yes."

In a previous experience, Matthews had felt that God had given to him an evangelism program for Southern Baptists. Once while in revival at Travis Avenue Church in Ft. Worth, with Hyman Appelman, an evangelist, Matthews was getting ready for a revival when

> God got my attention and laid a denominational program of evangelism on my heart. I shared it with Hyman. He thought it was great, but doubted if pastors would adopt it. Later when I was with Dr. Lawrence I was about to share the program with him when he said, "Wait a minute." He reached in his pocket and pulled out a piece of paper, saying, "Read this first." "So help me," Matthews said, "It was the same program. God had given it to him too."[120]

Matthews had no doubt the "Southern Baptist Program of Evangelism" was God's program. He defended and promoted it accordingly. An example of Matthews' personal dependence on prayer was illustrated one day when we were looking for a parking place in Nashville. He said as we circled the block, "I have gotten to where I unashamedly pray for a parking place." I answered that, "Now would be an appropriate time." Almost immediately a car pulled out of a parking place in front of us.[121]

Matthews had to retire because of poor health in 1955. All state conventions had full-time or part-time evangelism directors or were committed to it. Each convention had a statewide evangelism conference, and *The Southern Baptist Program of Evangelism* was the approved manual for evangelism in the denomination. The heart of the program was simultaneous revivals.

The 1955 simultaneous revivals campaign with the theme, "Every Church Revived in 55," was a nationwide effort resulting in the largest number of baptisms in Southern Baptist history—above 416,000.

C. E. Matthews must be credited with leading Southern Baptists into their first national program. When he retired in 1955, his successor, Leonard Sanderson, asked Matthews to continue in an advisory capacity. During the months before his death he went to the office in Dallas only once, but he and Sanderson visited together regularly, usually in Matthews's home.

In early 1955 Matthews made an appointment with Sanderson and told him that he was to be his successor. He felt God had revealed that to him. He told Sanderson that this was never before discussed with Courts Redford, executive secretary of the Home Mission Board. Sanderson requested and Matthews promised, that he never mention this to another person. Neither Matthews nor Sanderson ever mentioned this to another person, except their wives. At the time Matthews had thought he would continue until 1959. When his health began to fail and he notified Redford of his plans to retire Redford had asked for a suggestion about a successor. Matthews kept his promise to Sanderson and made no mention of a successor.

Sanderson was serving as evangelism director of the Tennessee Baptist Convention when Redford contacted him. He began his ministry with the Home Mission Board January 1, 1956, and continued until January 1, 1960.

Sanderson's philosophy was that the denominational program should coincide as nearly as possible with the local church program. Therefore, all church organizations should be involved in evangelism programs and promotion.

Before moving to Dallas, Sanderson met with heads of all departments and divisions of the Sunday School Board and they agreed on the church programs of evangelism involving church administrators, Sunday Schools, Training Union, and church music. The Sunday School Board also agreed to use their editorial department and all publications to work with the Home Mission Board evangelism program. The same kind of agreement was reached with the Brotherhood Commission, Women's Missionary Union, and the Radio and Television Commission.

Sanderson served as chairman of the "Baptist Jubilee Advance Committee" on evangelism with the participation of seven Baptist bodies in North America. In 1959 with a simultaneous effort Southern Baptists again broke all records in the number of baptisms, exceeding 429,000. Unfortunately this record was not to be exceeded until 1972.

Sanderson's emphasis was personal evangelism using the church organizations to promote it among the people. He wrote *Personal Soul-Winning* and *Using the Sunday School in Evangelism* study courses books promoted by the Training Union and Sunday School respectively.

During the Sanderson years, Vernon Yearby, a staff member, wrote the first *Evangelism Planbook* and Sanderson wrote the first *Associational Evangelism Workbook*. Members of C. E. Matthews's staff: C. Y. Dossey, Eual Lawson, E. Powell Lee, and C. E. Wilbanks, continued with Sanderson. Dossey promoted Mass Evangelism; Lawson, Associational Evangelism; and Yearby, after he joined the staff, local church evangelism.

When Sanderson resigned to become the pastor of First

Baptist Church, Lake Charles, Louisiana, he was asked to meet with Executive Secretary Court Redford and the personnel committee to suggest a successor. He suggested C. E. Autrey, professor of evangelism Southwestern Baptist Theological Seminary. Autry had previously served as evangelism director of the Louisiana Baptist Convention and then on Matthews's staff.

Sanderson later served several years as vocational evangelist, fifteen years as evangelism director in Louisiana and seven years visiting professor of Evangelism at Midwestern Baptist Theological Seminary, Kansas City. Sanderson also worked with the Southern Baptist Foreign Mission Board in evangelism projects in Taiwan, Argentina, and Mexico.

Autrey gave distinguished leadership in continuing a strong emphasis on simultaneous revivals and gave stronger emphasis to large centrally conducted area crusades than any other Southern Baptist leader. Two distinguished Matthews men, Dossey and Lawson, continued with Autrey. He also added two men whose names epitomize evangelism, John Havlik and Jack Stanton.

After some eight years of successful leadership, Autrey retired to again teach evangelism at Mid-America Baptist Seminary and New Orleans Baptist Seminary. He then served as a dynamic evangelism role model as pastor in Salt Lake City. Two of Autrey's most influential books are *Basic Evangelism* and *Revival in the O.T.*

Kenneth Chafin succeeded Autrey. Chafin taught evangelism at Southwestern Baptist Theological Seminary and headed the Billy Graham chair of evangelism at Southern Baptist Theological Seminary before going to the Home Mission Board.

Having already distinguished himself as a prolific writer and a popular preacher, Chafin made three unforgettable contributions to Southern Baptist evangelism: he led in breaking the baptismal record of 1959 and the convention baptized more people annually during his term than any previous leader. He also introduced the *Lay Evangelism School* method of teaching witnessing to laypersons. This approach continues to be the most effective method of training large numbers of Southern Baptist people in personal witnessing. This, or some similar approach, will likely be the most effective method of training people in the new *Marketplace Evangelism* emphasis among Southern Baptists. Third, Chafin introduced Lay Renewal as a Southern Baptist evangelism ministry with Reid Hardin as the effective leader.

Chafin's ministry as evangelism leader at the Home Mission Board was brief but dynamic. He left to become pastor of South Main Street Baptist Church in Houston, then back to Southern Baptist Theological Seminary to teach preaching. At this writing he is pastor of Walnut Street Baptist Church in Louisville.

C. B. "Bill" Hogue, former evangelism director for the Oklahoma Baptist Convention, succeeded Chafin. Just as Chafin had "baptized" some of the best of Campus Crusade and other para-church programs in developing the Lay Evangelism School, and made it adaptable to Southern Baptist churches, Hogue did the same by "baptizing" *Evangelism Explosion* into *Continued Witness Training* (CWT) and *Church Growth* into *Growing an Evangelistic Church.*

While many Southern Baptist churches continue to use para-church programs along with the Southern Baptist programs of evangelism, the programs Hogue introduced will be increasingly effective in Baptist churches.

Hogue also innovatively brought into evangelism some modern technological aids, apparently believing that "every good and perfect gift" is from above and God desires to use every possible method of enlisting as many people as possible to give the good news to as many people as possible, as soon as possible.

After fruitful and well-recognized leadership, Hogue went to a pastorate in Tulsa, Oklahoma. But his administrative "gifts" were again "freed up" as he became Executive Director of the California Southern Baptist Convention. Southern Baptist pastors baptized more people in the years under the leadership of Hogue than any other person that had served.

Robert L. Hamblin succeeded Hogue. Hamblin was teaching evangelism at New Orleans Seminary. Before that he had been pastor of Harrisburg Baptist Church in Tupelo, Mississippi, for more than twenty years. He had served as president of the Mississippi Baptist Convention and chaired some of the most strategic committees in the convention. Here are some quotes concerning Bob Hamblin from reputable evangelism leaders: "He was the most effective personal soul-winner of any pastor I ever knew." "He was the most practical and effective classroom teacher of evangelism I ever saw perform." "Hamblin is the best N.T. scholar ever to fill the position."

It may very well be that *Marketplace Evangelism,* begun during Hamblin's ministry, may become the most effective program (they say it is not a program, but it is, and correctly should be) in modern evangelism history.

In 1988, Hamblin resigned to head the Hancock Evangelism Foundation. This is a worldwide program of evangelism, involving many laypersons in innovative evangelism and contributes financially to other groups dedicated to evangelism. Hamblin continues a busy revival preaching schedule as well as the administrative leadership of the Hancock Foundation. He is called on to teach, preach, write, and otherwise contribute actively to world evangelism.

In May, 1988, Darrell Robinson, pastor of Dauphin Way Baptist Church in Mobile, Alabama, was elected director (vice president, Home Mission Board) to succeed Hamblin. He had distinguished himself as a dynamic church evangelism leader, both in Dauphin Way and First Baptist Church, Pasadena, Texas.

Robinson is giving wise counsel and leadership in conventional evangelism programs and promotion. His personal experience and leadership in Marketplace Evangelism are proving helpful and encouraging to the development of the new approach to lay participation in evangelism. During his first year Robinson has thoroughly mastered all programs and examined them in the light of his successful pastoral experience.

In his pastorate he enlisted and trained laypeople in witnessing and there are signs of a real revival of lay participation in all ministry, but especially evangelism. Each state convention has a strong department or division of evangelism with capable leadership. Any Southern Baptist pastor or church desiring help in developing a New Testament pattern of lay-led evangelism can get help in their state convention and Home Mission Board.

A recent survey of evangelism programs in most of the major denominations in America and abroad reveals a strong emphasis on personal evangelism with particular reference to lay participation. Numerous para-church groups have excellent helps available. The "Lausanne Committee" growing out of the Lausanne "Congress on World Evangelization" continues to make an everlasting global impact.

4
Ministry-based Evangelism

The church that would launch itself into the marketplace must do so using every evangelistic tool at its disposal. Many churches today are already experimenting with variations of evangelistic methodologies such as: thematic revival meetings, special evangelism events, varieties of personal evangelism training and lay-led programs designed to reach groups of people. One interesting approach that is being adopted by some churches is ministry-based evangelism or ministries based on a holistic approach to people and their needs.

Churches who take this approach point to Jesus' teaching about ministry to the multitudes. Jesus said, "Truly, I say to you, as you did it to one of the least of these my brethren, you did it to me" (Matt. 25:40). How is ministry-based evangelism accomplished? Is it for everyone? What makes it different?

The Calling

It is interesting that the passage in Matthew 25 is in the context of judgment. Matthew very clearly says that God will gather all the nations before Him and separate them—the just and unjust. His judgment seems to be based, in Matthew's gospel, on the ministries they performed or did not perform in Christ's name. Matthew seems to show us the heart of God for the needs of humanity in this passage. Certainly, Jesus' ministry focused on the totality of a person's need: to be saved, to be clothed, to be healed, to be forgiven of sins, for purpose in life . . . Scores of passages in the Scripture come to mind as Jesus dealt with the needs of people.

Certainly, every Christian can identify with Matthew's call for involvement in the lives of others just as Jesus' life became involved with others. When we are saved we are commissioned to follow Christ's example. His life-style was one of proclamation but also of ministry. To understand more fully what ministry means, we must define the term.

Robert Dale has given one definition of ministry. This definition certainly is at the base of this approach to evangelism. He says, "Ministry is words of witness to non-Christians. It is encouragement for the homeless, orphans, singles, aged, and formerly married. Ministry supports persons with fragmented emotions and fractured relationships. In short, ministry helps persons in Christ's name. The kinds of ministry actions are limited only by our vision and other's need."[122] This need can be as varied as individuals are varied. We must never try to treat all ministry needs the same. A sensitive heart will indicate how far ministry needs to go for each situation. Some will need a lot of help. Some will need less. We may well think it strange to talk about ministry to the wealthy but the wealthy need support, love, caring and compassion just like those who are poor. So ministry cuts across all lines. It is care and concern for the wealthy, the poor, the happy, the discouraged, the successful, those who are confident in themselves, those who need Jesus as their Savior.

Therefore as Christ ministered to others, rich and poor, so should we. His ministry touched human need. For example, He healed. Can we heal? Certainly we can aid in healing. There are hosts of people who cannot afford decent medical care. Can the Christian community help by providing financially for a doctor's care for these who otherwise would have no way to pay the costs? Or can Christian doctors help by donating a portion of their services during the week to those who cannot pay?

I remember when I was in seminary.[123] I was as poor as could be. My wife and I barely made enough money to pay our rent. When our little girl was born the doctor who delivered her never billed us for the delivery. He knew our plight, not because I told him. I never mentioned our financial position to him. He helped us because he volunteered his time weekly to helping seminary students with their medical needs. He was a marketplace minister.

I know a golf pro who takes time to counsel people who have needs and who play golf at his club.[124] He went through training in Christian counseling just so he could help others. Could carpenters, lawyers, nurses, and so on volunteer a portion of their time and their skills weekly for the poor and needy or for those who have burdens? And could the church help coordinate that volunteer work? Why not?

Sure there are risks. Churches and individual Christians might be taken advantage of. But the Scripture doesn't tell us to minister only in those situations where we will be guaranteed that no one will take advantage of us. Not long ago, I sat in a business meeting in a church where the debate centered on ministering to a refugee family.[125] The church members argued among themselves more about the liability the church might incur than talk about the opportunity to claim a lost family for Christ. They lost the joy of being ministering evangelists.

Recently, I served in a church as interim pastor. One Sunday evening a man appeared in the church office shortly before the service was to begin. He told me that he was cold, hungry, and had no place to live. He indicated that he had spent the last two nights sleeping outside under a tree near

our church. The chairman of deacons and I arranged to give
him shelter for three nights so that he could rest and report
for a job he had later in the week.

My wife and I carried him food during those three days and
on each occasion I witnessed to him of God's care and love
and of our church's care and love for him. He heard the gospel daily. I arranged for a businessman in the church to pick
up the gentleman on the day he was to report for work since
he did not own a car. When the businessman arrived, the
man had left town. Did he take advantage of our generosity
and our ministry? Yes, he did. But does that mean we failed?
He was ministered to in Jesus' name—fed, clothed, given
shelter, and presented the gospel of Jesus Christ. We had
sowed seeds. And the promise of the Scripture is that those
seeds will not die but sprout one day in his heart. We don't
always have the results we want in our ministry efforts.
Sometimes we get disappointed. But we still minister.

In the course of marketplace evangelism you will discover
needs. Unfortunately, we have become so specialized in our
theological positions that we categorize priorities into ministry, evangelism, and missions. The early church knew no
such distinction.

The Christian world is sometimes separated into two
camps; those who are given to social ministry—the cup of
cold water in Jesus' name and those who are directly confron-
tational in their approach to evangelism. Churches even spe-
cialize in ministry or evangelism with their logos. One will
say it is a church "centered on meeting needs" while another
is a church that "proclaims the gospel." And it is even more
unfortunate that we sometimes talk or preach as if ministry
and evangelism are opposed to each other. Ministry and
evangelism are like the railroad track. The train needs both

rails to travel forward. Even so, we need ministry and evangelism if our churches are to travel forward for Christ.

People sometimes criticize social ministry for not being
concerned enough with regard to a person's lostness. And
those in social ministry sometimes criticize evangelists for
not being sensitive to the needs of people. But there is no
need for such criticism. Some denominations have been especially sensitive in both areas. We have often reacted instead of evaluated our opportunities. When we simply react
we can make some unfortunate choices.

According to Findley Edge,

> One of the reasons Southern Baptists have emphasized per-
> sonal salvation and tended to minimize social involvement
> was based on a theological perspective. In the latter part of
> the last century and the early part of this century, a rather
> large segment of Protestantism began to emphasize nurture
> as the normal mode by which individuals entered the king-
> dom of God rather than through a conversion experience.
> Other issues were involved, but this was one of the key is-
> sues. Southern Baptists rejected this "liberal" theology.
> About the same time these same churches also began a
> rather vigorous ministry to social needs of the poor and out-
> cast. Southern Baptists tended to identify this social minis-
> try with the liberal theology. Because they rejected the
> liberal theology, they also rejected the social concern.[126]

But more and more Southern Baptist churches are becoming
ministry minded.

These churches have found that social ministry and evangelism belong together. They are not mutually exclusive of
one another. Some denominations have learned the hard way
that it is impossible to separate the two. The early church
knew that it took both. Acts 6 is all about meeting needs and

reaching people for Christ. It is interesting that one of the most notable evangelists in the New Testament, Phillip, was also one charged with ministry to the needs of those around him (Acts 6). And certainly no one could dispute the life of Stephen, also chosen by the church and charged to minister, with an evangelistic witness that cost him his life!

Matthew's gospel is replete with examples of evangelistic ministry in the marketplace. Chapters 8 through 10 illustrate the ministry of Jesus to the poor and to the rich. He healed the leper—one with no social position—and then by contrast the servant of one with social position—a Roman centurion. Jesus ministered to Peter's mother-in-law, those possessed with demons, a scribe, and Matthew, the tax collector. A ruler came to Jesus with his daughter's need and in the process of going to her a poor woman touched Jesus and was healed. On and on Jesus ministered to the broad spectrum of human need. The rich needed Jesus as much as the poor. Certainly this ought to be the pattern for our ministry today.

If we look at history carefully, we will see that social ministry and evangelism go hand in glove. In fact, in the early days of this country when revival was sweeping every town, social ministry was its natural outgrowth. Schools, orphanages, hospitals, poor houses, and other relief agencies had their start as the result of the Great Awakening in this country. The evangelists of the revival period between about 1830 and 1865 provide the answer to this whole question about social ministry and evangelism.

In a book by Timothy L. Smith, *Revivalism and Social Reform,* attention is called to the fact that during the revivals of the mid-1800s the evangelists were among the leaders in social reform and ministry. "The loss of this knowledge has been tragic for both evangelical reform and for society."[127]

Certainly, it is time for us to return to an aggressive approach to ministry-based evangelism.

Ministry-based evangelism ought to be the norm of every Christian's life today. And it should be the door of opportunity for every church. Just how do you define ministry-based evangelism? *It is loving and ministering to people at the point of their need and confronting them with the claims of Christ, who can meet that need, so that people will accept Christ and then minister to others.*[128]

One pastor has made it very clear in his church's direction how they will approach ministry-based evangelism. He said, "We tell everyone we find, 'We are here to help you. We love you and we want to meet your need. If you don't make a decision for Christ we are still going to love you and minister to you because we want you to have more than a plate of food or clothes on your back. We want you to have life. And the only way you are going to have life is through Jesus Christ.'"[129] That kind of approach is the heart of ministry-based evangelism.

The Concept

Many churches across America could adopt ministry-based evangelism as a basic foundation to reaching people. Why? Because all people everywhere have needs. Physical needs rank very high on the scale of need. If we did little else than minister to the poverty stricken, certainly we would have a full-time task at hand.

Poverty rears its ugly head all over the world and in affluent America in every community. One of seven Americans now live below the poverty level. Women and children account for 78 percent of those in poverty.[130] In Atlanta, some 8,000 are homeless and in Texas 800,000 go hungry some part of each month.[131] Although this book is not written to give statistics on poverty as its goal, any reading of books in this area will stagger our thoughts. The problem is serious. Poverty touches us all. More and more people are appearing on the street corner with signs that proclaim, "I will work for food."

There are hundreds of county-seat towns with large churches, especially in the South. These churches could provide shelters for the homeless, and do a lot to feed the poor. The shame of our day is that every winter people freeze to death on the streets of major cities because they cannot get into shelters. And most every downtown church in these cities is locked up tight every night. Could we begin to see that the church ought to be used every day for reaching people and not just on Sunday? When are we going to unlock our churches and take in those people who cannot help themselves especially during the cold of winter? Some of the most prime real estate that could be available to the poor and homeless is found in our unused and locked church facilities.

In most large cities it is very likely that enough food is thrown away daily by fast-food restaurants to feed the homeless and hungry in those cities. Many cafeteria-style restaurants overcook amounts of food that have to be destroyed every day. Could the churches coordinate the feeding of those people and use the surplus food that no one eats?

Many thousands of young women become pregnant each year and have abortions. Is it possible for churches to provide an alternative to abortion through loving Christian counseling? What about pregnancy-care centers sponsored by a loving church that could counsel a young woman and help her find another way to deal with her pregnancy than through the tragedy of abortion? And what about Christian homes that would help shelter her until her baby is born so that she would have the support of a loving family? Why not help these young women turn their pregnancy from a terrible problem to an event of happiness based on Christ and His care for all persons?

There is a church in Florida that has demonstrated this kind of concern for years. First Baptist Church, Leesburg, Florida, has consistently baptized hundreds of people using a ministry-based evangelism approach. They have also retained a large percentage of those baptized. They have discipled them and trained many to share their faith.

As of 1990 this church had ministries which include: a pregnancy care center, a men's transient shelter, a women's shelter, a children's shelter, a counseling service, ministry to homebound, and an active bus ministry. Each ministry is directed by laypersons who have given their lives to the ministry. Over a thousand individuals have been touched by the ministry of this church. And hundreds have been led to Jesus.

Ministry-based evangelism is a possibility for every church who wants to reach people for Christ. While it may not take on the larger dimensions of a First Baptist Church there is no reason why many churches could not learn to respond to the social needs of the community and understand that evangelism is a part of that need ministry. After all, our gospel witness can take on real dimensions of love as we grow closer and get "hands-on" experience with those who need Jesus.

The Commitment

What does it take to get started? Commitment. It's really that simple. The church must be led to the place where it makes a commitment to reach its community regardless of the kind of people it encounters. It must understand that God has called us to redemptive ministry and evangelism. To be redemptive in today's world will mean evangelizing the lost, feeding the hungry, giving shelter to the poor and homeless, helping the wealthy find purpose in Christ, seeking to help an unwed mother and involvement with social agencies in the larger community that need the extension of service that a church can give.

Once a commitment is made a church can set up a program using gifted people in the church whose experience as businesspersons in the marketplace contribute to the development of the ministries. These laypersons know how to get the ministries underway. Why not bring their marketplace gifts of business into the church and tap that rich source? They can help organize resources, personnel, and finances necessary to minister.

Recently, I spoke on tithing to a small-membership church.[132] One person in the congregation came to me after the service and told me that the reason he felt most people did not tithe was because they never saw where the money was going. My immediate reaction was that this was a poor excuse. But then I rethought. *Perhaps he is right. Maybe our eyes of faith need a few concrete examples. After all, in many churches it seems the money goes to a lot of maintenance kinds of activities rather than ministry.* I suspect that in those churches that do ministry-based evangelism more people are inclined to give to reach the needs of the community. In fact, the pastor of one church doing ministry-based evangelism told me that his church was nearly ten thousand dollars ahead of budget because the people had gotten so excited about reaching their community for Christ and ministering to the needs all around them.

Delos Miles has suggested a number of ways to construct outreach strategies that can be used to minister to people and reach them with the gospel.[133] Obviously, these suggestions would have to be tailor-designed for the individual church and its community. A church would have to examine local restrictions, laws, zoning, and other such legal matters. But to the church willing to minister in the community, these are small obstacles. Experience has also shown that businessmen and other laypersons are often in the know about such things and can help churches with the design of such programs. Indeed, they should take the lead and model lay involvement in the ministries. A few suggestions for ministry might include:

Ministry to the poor and hungry.
Support groups for persons coping with tragedy or various life transitions.
Evangelism training for laypersons.
Alcohol- and drug-education workshops.
Counseling offered to the community by Christian psychologists and sponsored by your church.
Bible studies and prayer groups in the workplace.
Shopping-center chaplains sponsored by local churches.
Industrial chaplains.
Political action groups to implement Christian social concerns.
Ministries centered around recreation areas.
Marriage and family support groups and seminars.
Literacy classes.

These are just a few ideas that a church might explore to minister to its community.[134] After all, ministry need not occur only at church on Sunday morning. It should take place on Mondays, Saturdays, Tuesdays, or whenever people come into contact with loving and caring Christians who want to carry the message of Christ to the lost world.

It is so easy for a church to turn its eyes inward and focus its attention on itself. How many hundreds of churches have built facilities designed to meet the fellowship and recreation needs of its members but have never really used them to reach the lost community? The unchurched are unlikely to beg us for a gospel witness. We will have to go to them and make some radical approaches to the community if we are to win them to Jesus and minister in His name. Perhaps the story told in Matthew 25 is told to help us get our eyes on Jesus and on a lost world. When we do that we will begin as a popular Christian song says, ". . . stop carrying water to the ocean and start carrying it to the desert."[135]

5
The Church in the Marketplace

In this book, we are thinking of all the church as including all the people of God. We are thinking of the marketplace as the arena of life in which people live out their lives. Therefore the marketplace includes the school, the workplace, the home place, the recreation place, or wherever people live their lives in relation to others. Since the church is God's people wherever they are, they are God's people during the weekday in the workplace as well as the Sunday place.

Unfortunately, the church has often been heard saying, "When you come to God and into the church you come out of the world. The church is pure and clean and the world is impure and dirty." The admonition, "be ye separate," has sounded like, "Stay out of that old sinful world. Make your friends of holy people and stay away from all those old mean people with whom you associated before you became a Christian. Unfortunately, you may have to go back to the marketplace to make a living, but don't touch it any more than you have to."

It has sounded like the church was saying on Sunday night, "Go home, take off the Sunday clothes and hang them in the cedar-lined closet of protection from the old evil workplace so they will not be contaminated. Go on to the workplace and do what you have to do, but don't bring it here. Take off the world clothes and go back to the Sunday clothes

when you come back to church next Sunday." We haven't
meant to say that, but it has sometimes sounded like that.
The problem has been that church has too often been
thought of as the Sunday place and the workplace as the
world place.

For years people like Elton Trueblood, in many books, and
Findley Edge, in books like *The Greening of the Church* and
The Doctrine of the Laity,[136] have been reminding us that on
Sunday we are the gathered church and during the week we
are the scattered church. The people of God are the people of
God whether toting their tithes and offerings down the aisle
of the meeting house or counting the filthy lucre at the bank.
We are learning that pulpit and pew furniture do not make a
place sacred and store counters do not make a place carnal.
It is the people in both places who decide whether or not the
place they stand is holy ground. God desires holiness in both
places because he desires holiness in our lives wherever we
are.

Ministry in the Marketplace

No doctrine of the New Testament is clearer than the doctrine of servanthood. Jesus practiced servanthood and taught
it to his disciples. One of the words Jesus used to describe
what he practiced and preached was *diakoneo*, "to minister"
"to serve" (see Luke 22:26-27; John 12:2,26). Forms of the
same word are used to aescribe ministry in the familiar story
of the apostles' selection of people to serve tables while they
continued to give attention to prayer and the ministry of the
word. The same word was used to describe the apostles' work
and that of the newly selected "deacon" (see Acts 6:1,2,4). So
it is unfortunate that the scriptural word for *minister* has been
professionalized to refer to pastors only.

Indeed, pastors are *ministers, servants,* but according to

the typical New Testament (and Old Testament) use of the term, all God's people are *ministers*. So, ministry in the marketplace is service in the marketplace. If it is Christian service it is Christian ministry. So *ministry* is a word with broad implications and definitions. We are here emphasizing one particular form of ministry. This work is about evangelism ministry, not to the disparagement of other ministries, but this happens to be an evangelism book. We are writing about evangelism ministry according to the New Testament use of the word evangelism as "good news" (see page 00). Furthermore it should be explained that evangelism ministries do not preclude other Christian ministries by the same person at the same time.

Jesus never seemed to have any problems with duality of evangelism and other ministries. Sometimes He met physical or mental needs of people without any known evangelism needs being met. Sometimes He met all those kinds of needs in ministering to the same person. Sometimes He began with one kind of ministry, sometimes the other. Would it not seem that He would likely insist on the same kind of mixture of ministries today in our marketplace as He did in His marketplace then? He performed ministries as He saw needs.

Jesus did seem to follow certain ministry principles. First, He seemed to minister to the person who needed Him most urgently. At the pool of Bethesda there "lay a multitude of invalids, blind, lame, paralyzed." But note there was, "One man there, who had been ill for thirty-eight years." Jesus ministered to that man (see John 5:3,5). Second, Jesus ministered to the need which was most urgent. When He saw sick people, He healed them (see Matt. 14:14). When He saw hungry people, He fed them (see Matt. 15:32-37). When He saw two blind men, He gave them their sight (see Matt. 20:33,34). When He saw a bereaved widow, He raised her son from the dead (Luke 7:12-15). When He saw a sinful woman, He forgave her sins (see John 4:5-30). When Jesus entered Jericho, with all the crowds there, He saw Zacchaeus in his sins and said, "Today has salvation come to this house" (see Luke 19:1-10). So Jesus met urgent needs with immediate ministry.

There are many people, Christians and non-Christians, who meet people's physical and emotional needs every day at the marketplace. Our present plea is that we Christians who have learned how Christ meets our needs, share this ministry with the same respect and discretion.

Evangelism Ministry in the Marketplace

Two members of the governor's staff were traveling halfway across the state from a political meeting when one of them said, "Joe, you know I've never had too much patience with some of our Christian friends, but if I could be the kind you are, I think I would consider it." Joe had been praying for an opportunity to witness to his friend, but was taken by such surprise he was speechless. Now he was embarrassed that he didn't know what to say. There was a seemingly endless silence except for the car and the road noise.

"I'm sorry, I didn't mean to embarrass you," Joe's friend apologized. When Joe finally recovered his voice he said, "No, Spence, you see if I'm embarrassed, it's because, in the first place, I know I don't deserve it; in the second place I don't want to get in a position of preaching to you, because I am not as good a Christian as I ought to be."

"Man, don't put yourself down," Joe's friend interrupted. "If I could be the kind of Christian you are, I'd do it in a minute, but that's just not me. I'm sorry."

"Spence," Joe laughingly answered, "it's not me either. You see, the Bible which is the only thing we have to go by says

God wants you and me both to be Christians, and it also says that neither one of us deserves it. Furthermore, it says that neither of us can do it by ourselves. You know, Spence, it was a big surprise to me, I guess because I had never thought about it, that God wants us all to be His children." Joe went on, "It came out the other Sunday in a Sunday school class discussion. It was somewhere in the Bible that it is not God's will that any should perish, but that all should come to repentance. It was also pointed out that all of us sin. Of course, I know I do. But this teacher, you know, is a pretty neat guy. He read to us that Jesus paid the fine for our sins and offers us salvation as a gift."

Just at that moment Spence drove into Joe's driveway. "Well, we'll have to talk about this some more one of these days, Joe. It at least made the trip seem a little shorter to have something interesting to talk about. You get a good night's sleep, at least what's left of it. I'll see you, Friend." Joe knew it was time to get out of the car.

The next morning Joe stuck a little booklet in his pocket. He had received it in a special training event at his church. The booklet was designed to be read to someone whom you are trying to help become a Christian. At first, after the training course Joe had carried one of the booklets in his pocket for just such an occasion. Now that he didn't have it, he needed it. *Well, I couldn't have read it to him very well in the car anyway,* he reasoned. *Maybe I will get a chance to at least give him the booklet today.*

Instead, it seemed that Spence evaded him for three days. He barely spoke as Joe passed him in the office lobby. Finally Joe decided that as a Christian he must take the initiative. He knocked on Spence's office door, deliberately passing the secretary's desk.

"Come on in," Spence called out; then looked more than

disappointed when Joe opened the door. "Have a seat, Joe?"—more a question than an invitation. Then shuffling papers on his desk, he asked, "What's on your mind, Joe?"

"I'm not going to take your time, Spence. I can see you are busy. I have this little booklet here that I think will answer some of the questions we discussed the other night. All I want you to do is read it, particularly in the light of what you said that you have thought the Christian life might be for you. I'm not going to bug you. Just allow yourself about fifteen minutes and give it a good reading, OK?"

"OK, I'll do it, Joe," he smiled. "Anything else?" he asked, as he slipped the booklet in his pocket. "That's all, Spence. Thank you," he smiled as he gently closed the door. Joe told his wife, Sue, the story and they discussed how they might bring Spence's wife in on the action. A few weeks later in a party at the governor's mansion, Sue deliberately sat by Janet at an informal moment. They hit it off well together in conversation. As the conversation was ending Sue said, "Jan, we need to get together. Joe really admires and respects Spence." She got an enthusiastic, "I'd like that, and I'm sure Spence would."

In about a week Sue called Janet and invited them to the football game and dinner afterwards. Following a reciprocal invitation and some subsequent conversation, Spence and Jan joined Sue and Joe in church one night for a special musical program. Following several visits to the church and some more relaxed conversation, Spence suggested that Jan call the pastor and ask if he would come and answer some questions for them. They are now as regular in attendance as Joe and Sue. Spence is actually a little more forthright in witnessing to others than Joe. By the way, they thought it was real neat that the pastor had them in the baptismal pool together and made their baptism a kind of joint ceremony.

Frequently, the marketplace evangelism opportunity grows out of some other ministry, like ministering to someone sick, or even a kind deed in some business experience.

How to Be a Marketplace Evangelist

It is interesting, but true, that young people seem to practice marketplace evangelism more easily than older people. They don't seem to possess the same fears or hangups. Yet another similar discovery has been made: people with a less vigorous religious upbringing often have less embarrassment in informal witnessing to others, once they have become Christians. Why would people inexperienced in religious work be less backward in talking about the Christian experience?

The answer seems to lie in the fact that some have to unlearn before they can learn. Some people who grew up in church were influenced, or in some cases, victimized by perversions and fanaticism in witnessing. A very small handful of charlatans and misinformed zealots have prevented a lot of otherwise capable and dedicated people from witnessing. There have also been the door-to-door visitors, with basically poor Bible backgrounds, who have memorized a presentation with twisted and perverted words, who try to overpower the vulnerable. Some good people have refused to do legitimate conversational evangelism because they didn't want to be like some fanatics they had seen.

Why would it be more difficult to talk with a friend about her or his relationship to the Lord than about a job at the place where you work? Why would it be more difficult to talk with a person about the Lord than about a new health program you have learned about? If you have ever doubted the reality of a devil who tries to interfere with and impede our Christian lives, the above questions might give you a clue.

Admitting we have a problem, how can we deal with it?

1. Pray. Praying is the heart of any genuine desire to help others become Christians. Our praying begins with sincere thanksgiving to God for providing salvation in the first place. Then we thank Him for those who helped us know how to become Christians. They may have been pastors, maybe friends, or maybe just someone from the church who had enough commitment to do that which may have been just as difficult for them as for us.

After sincere thanksgiving, ask God to remove your fears and hangups or give you courage in spite of them. We need to pray that God will remove from our minds the success/failure syndrome. We need to ask God for the ability to have relaxed conversation with people, just as relaxed as if we are talking about something else.

2. Practice talking with people about nonreligious subjects. Initiate conversations about interesting subjects. Then when you are alone, recall the conversation and remember how easy, even how pleasant it was to initiate a conversation.

3. Practice initiating conversations that include some religious, but non-threatening, conversation. Remember you are simply trying to learn to talk to another person about the Lord as easily and naturally as about any other subject.

4. Make a list of people you would like to see become Christians. They may be people where you work, live, play, go to school, or people in your neighborhood. Keep the list where you have easy access to it, preferably where you can see it several times a day. Simply add to the list as you think of them. Set aside a certain time of day to pray for them. Pray for any of their needs you may be aware of, but especially that they will become Christians.

5. Look for opportunities to be helpful and kind (not patronizing or gushy). Just be a genuine good neighbor in every possible way.

6. *If your church has a marketplace evangelism ministry, get involved in it.* If your church does not have such a program, talk with the pastor and other leaders about starting one. Do not be a complainer; be a Christian leader. All of the above things you can do in marketplace evangelism, whether anyone else does or not. As a matter of fact, if you will do the above things in a spirit of prayer and love, you will have the fastest growth as a Christian you have experienced. Furthermore, you can do most of the things discussed in the following pages, even if nobody else does. However, somebody else will!

7. *Review the necessary scriptural information about how one actually becomes a Christian.* Ask your pastor or someone for some written material. Learn what to say if someone asks, "How do you become a Christian?" "How can you know you are a Christian?" It will amaze you how soon you will be able to use it.

The Pastor as Evangelism Equipper

Pastors love evangelism. Have you ever known one who was not happy when people were becoming Christians? Pastors' life-styles, like others, are shaped by their backgrounds and experiences. For example there is nothing about the call to be a pastor or the ordination that equips some to be an evangelist. Pastors and others are evangelistic because they *become* evangelistic. Some pastors found it easier to be evangelistic pastors because they had a good model along the way. Some were turned off to evangelism, unfortunately, because of a bad model. But all pastors love to see people receive eternal life. These pages are written with the hope that they will be helpful to some pastors in their evangelistic ministry.

The Pastor as Leader

While the New Testament seems clear in its teaching that all God's people are to be ministers, it is also clear that God calls and gifts some to be leaders. Different English words are used to translate the Greek word *episkopes,* or some form of it, in 1 Tim. 1:1,2; Acts 20:28; Phil. 1:1; Titus 1:7. However, by precept and example the New Testament teaches the need for strong, dynamic leadership. The very principle of "all the people of God" participating in evangelism in the life of the church demands strong leadership by the pastor (and staff where applicable). We are not talking about dictatorship. Not a lot of brains or spirituality are required to be a dictator. A lot of both are required to be a strong, dynamic, evangelism leader. This kind of leader is secure in his calling and relationship with God. He loves people and knows how to get along with them. He knows the role of the pastor and is sure of his own objectives and goals in this particular church. He is following the Pauline doctrine of leadership (see Eph. 4:11*ff*).

The Pastor as Evangelist

To be an evangelism leader the pastor must have some personal objectives and goals in evangelism. If he does, he will practice them.

In the first place he will be a personal evangelist. This expresses itself privately and publicly. You may have known some pastors who seemed evangelistic enough in their sermons, but never had a known conversation with a live prospect. This might indicate more interest in preaching than people. On the other hand, if a pastor is genuinely interested enough in seeing people become Christians that he works at it personally, he will eventually become a good communicator of the message publicly. Without a doubt, the best preparation for effective evangelistic preaching are prayer and personal witnessing. Obviously, if the pastor leads the way and sets an example in personal evangelism, he can lead others more effectively.

Secondly, evangelistic preaching is necessary, both for immediate evangelistic results, and for leading and training people in evangelism. This is true both of the sermon and the invitation. Now good evangelistic preaching does not consist of mere loudness, length, and lather. It is not of necessity defensive, disputatious, nor dull. It is neither silly, simplistic, nor superficial. A member of the pastor–search committee said, "We have had an evangelistic pastor. I think we now need a teacher-type."

His perception was limited. I think he was saying, "We have had sound. We now need substance." I don't see any conflict between evangelism and teaching. Evangelistic preaching is informative, interesting, and inspiring. The hearer must receive the truth itself. It needs to be interesting enough to command his attention, and inspiring enough to capture his will. Even though a person has made a personal commitment to Jesus in a private setting, it is still not easy to walk down that church aisle in front of people. The invitation needs to be clear, charismatic, and candid. The evangelistic pastor must practice and preach evangelism.

The Pastor as a Planner

The pastor is not a mere performer. The words, *overseer, shepherd, pastor, leader, bishop* indicate responsibility. A pastor complained to the seminar leader, "I like what you say about growing an evangelistic church. I believe in evangelism and I want my church to be evangelistic, but it's this strong, assertive leadership that bothers me. I played football. When the people applauded I would risk breaking all my bones to get that ball across that line. If my members would applaud me I would be the best pastor they ever had, but this matter of strong, assertive, responsible leadership bugs me. That's not my style."

The seminar leader answered as you would expect. He explained: "You are not now just a player on the field. You are the coach. You have to plan the plays and inspire the players. The crowd applauds when you win. They almost deify you. But let you have a few losses and the same people boo you. You must be a strong leader when you are winning and a stronger leader when you are losing.

The evangelistic leader studies, teaches, and preaches the Bible to be sure the divine directives are sound. He surveys and studies the field to understand the opportunities and responsibilities of the church. He prayerfully scrutinizes the church roll to ascertain the ministry potential of the members. Evangelistic leadership includes specific location of prospects, where they live, work, go to school, shop, play. (Are we serious about this business?) Your state denominational office will provide help with the details.

Evangelistic leadership involves matching up members with prospects. Where are the lost people in the community? They are in the shops, stores, offices, schools, factories, neighborhoods, and homes. Where are the people of God who comprise our churches? They are in the shops, stores, offices, schools, factories, neighborhoods, and homes.

There are several possible ways of matching up the people of God with those to be ministered to: 1. At the workplace or school place; 2. In the neighborhoods; and 3. In the Sunday school age group or other church organization. All three matches should be made simultaneously. (Again, are we serious about this business?)

In the case of professional groups like doctors or lawyers, there are different kinds of groupings: doctors may be placed in hospital groups, or with a small medical group; lawyers might be placed in a courthouse group or a small legal group, independent business people might be placed in small business groups. There are additional groupings like women's clubs, garden clubs, golfing clubs, fishing or hunting clubs, civic clubs, unions, and professional organizations.

Some churches will have all of these groupings. Some churches will not have nearly so many, and some will have groups we have not mentioned. An assignment and report system will be devised with proper report forms and designated times for reports to be given to designated people. When someone has been reached the report system will be coordinated so that all members who have that prospect will be informed. At this point the newly reached person would be placed into the proper discipleship group.

The paperwork should not even be discussed with workers until the assignments are made. At that time the proper form will be given to the proper people. Never allow the logistics to become the substitute for ministry or to scare people off.

All the people of God who participate should be thoroughly trained. Well-qualified people will be given the training responsibility for each ministry group. A One-Day Soul-Winning Workshop could be ideally adapted to this (Contact your state Evangelism office).

The Pastor and Prayer Planning

Where this program is launched on a churchwide basis, the pastor should plan a month of prayer participation. Every person involved and every phase of the program should be bathed in prayer. There should be special prayer meetings, special prayer times in regular prayer meetings, prayers in worship services and special people, like shut-ins, enlisted in prayer. Where the program is not launched on a churchwide basis, but by smaller units, appropriate prayer programs should be provided. Remember, most people pray when they are enlisted to pray. All churches can qualify for some phase of this ministry, regardless of background and previous training.

How many paid staff people will be needed to coordinate and manage this program? Ideally, none. Our churches are filled with people who are gifted, and many of them trained for this kind of administrative ministry. In a large church an administrative or steering committee will coordinate the entire program. In smaller churches, obviously fewer people will be involved. Most of the people needed to manage the program are not involved in the church program at all now. Remember that about 20 percent of the people are doing the church work now. Most of our members have never been asked to do anything in the church except attend and give. Don't expect volunteers to begin with. They are not accustomed to that and will not respond to that yet. The people will have to be asked. But they will respond.

Don't neglect the faithful people who have been doing all the other church work, like leaders and workers in all the organizations, finance committees, ushers, etc. We cannot get along without them. By all means you do not want them to feel they are being forgotten. Enlist their prayers and support, but enlist mainly the people.

Pastor/Staff Relations in Marketplace Evangelism

All church ministries and programs should be worked out jointly between pastor and all professional staff people. This is especially true with a churchwide ministry like market-place evangelism. If the pastor or some other staff member is thoroughly acquainted with marketplace evangelism, that person may present it to the entire staff. In some cases it might be desirable to bring in some marketplace evangelism person to present the concept to the entire group, even though the pastor or some other staff member is knowledge-able. The subject should be covered thoroughly. All questions should be cleared. In some ways this may become one of the most revolutionary changes in church ministries in centuries.

We have always talked about need for all the people of God to be involved in all work of God. This direction can bring it to fruition. Nobody will question that this is New Testament Christianity. It must not be "the pastor's program," it must be the church ministering. All age groups will be involved. For example, the entire concept, as it relates to them, should be carefully explained to youth. So you see, every grouping in the church should be oriented. There should be a solid front from the staff. Agree to be positive and enthusiastic. Don't launch it as a churchwide program until the staff is ready. You might begin the program with one or more small groups, like youth, or professional groups, without everybody's coop-eration, then later enlarge it when you are ready.

Most programs fail before they begin because proper prep-aration has not been made. Usually, failure is because of a lack of prayer or a lack of information. All churches do not need multiple staffs, and no church needs a disjointed staff.

The Pastor and Staff as Equippers

Jesus was an equipper. The philosophy of Jesus seemed to be that all the people of God behaving like the people of God will result in more people becoming the people of God. The strategy of Jesus for teaching people is people. At the very beginning of His ministry He began the selection and training of ordinary people as disciples (Gr. *mathetes,* learner, taught ones, trained ones, or if female, *mathetria*).

He not only trained His disciples through special teaching sessions, but His preferred method seemed to be that they were *with Him, watched Him,* and *listened to Him* as He taught in the synagogues, preached the gospel of the kingdom, healed all kinds of diseases, and fed the hungry. Then the time came when He gave them special instructions and sent them out on ministry assignments. They came back and reported, sometimes to be affirmed, and sometimes reprimanded. After some more learning, there were sent out again, along with others.

The evangelism plan of Jesus is people. Isn't that the reason He went into the church business in the first place? Isn't that the ground for the wide-open commissions to all His people to reach out to all people with the good news? (see Matt. 28:19-20).

Paul was an equipper. It would be difficult to imagine the New Testament without names like Luke, Barnabas, Aquila, Priscilla, and many, many others who worked with Paul in the ministry of the churches, in the new church starts, to say nothing of those who were left as leaders in the churches as Paul moved on.

Peter, who was a slow learner about God being no respecter of persons, finally wrote,

> . . . you are a chosen race, a royal priesthood, a holy nation, God's own people, that you may declare the wonderful deeds of him who called you out of darkness into his marvelous light. Once you were no people but now you are God's people . . . (1 Pet. 2:9-10).

So the emerging pattern is one in which the pastor (and staff, where applicable) would pray and dream concerning possible evangelism ministries in the community. He (they) would share those prayers and dream with other responsive church leaders, and enlist their dreams and prayers. They might then begin to arrange groupings of people in the community who need to be reached.

The next step would be pulling up the names of church members who are already in these same groups. They would be called together, enlisted, and trained to begin the ministry. The pastor (staff) dreams and prays, then shares their dreams and prayers with some leaders. These leaders share their dreams and prayers. The leaders lead out in many of the preparation details, while the pastor (staff) leads, prepares, equips, teaches, and guides.

The People of God as Ministers

Paul gave a clear statement concerning the relationship between pastor and people in ministry. If you read Ephesians 4:11-16 in the following translations: *New English Bible, Good News Bible, The Jerusalem Bible, New American Standard Bible,* and *New International Version,*[137] you will find that the changing of a comma from the KJV and several other translations clearly shows that the primary role of pastoral leaders is equipping all the people of God as ministers.

Here it is in the *Good News Bible:*

> It was he who "gave gifts to mankind"; he appointed some to be apostles, others to be prophets, others to be evangelists, others to be pastors and teachers. He did this to prepare all God's people for the work of Christ service . . . .

The meaning would then be that the ministries (apostles, prophets, evangelists, pastors, and teachers) of verse 11 are

given in order that the saints be equipped for the work of services which belongs to the whole body. Dr. W. O. Carver
translated it similarly ". . . with a view to the perfecting of
the saints unto (such maturity and equipment and, devotion
that they would all be engaged properly in) a work of service . . ."[138]

Sample Church
(In Marketplace Evangelism)

Fictitious names will be used for the church and marketplace entities. Our purpose is to outline some of the preliminary steps in launching a churchwide marketplace evangelism
ministry. The ministry might be much larger and more inclusive, but we are illustrating the simplest marketplace approach to evangelism ministry.

The community used in the sample is a suburban community, comprising a part of a total community of some 70,000
people. This is a preliminary outline and work sheet which
becomes much more refined as the program develops.

Magnolia Baptist Church
Fictitious, Arkansas

The marketplace ministry began as a result of the pastor
calling together a hand-picked group of members for spiritual brainstorming. One of the presentations to the group for
consideration was by a person with some background study
and work in marketplace evangelism. A study group was appointed to work with the pastor and staff and make a report
to a joint meeting of Church Council, deacons, and other
church members. In that joint meeting there was a vote to
recommend to the church that they launch a marketplace
ministry with evangelism being the primary thrust, but with
the understanding that the ministry spread in whatever directions needed in the future.

It was agreed that the deacon chairman would make a presentation of the proposal to the church at the close of a Sunday morning service (well-announced in advance), that a Wednesday night business meeting might be used for congregational discussion, with the pastor and staff participating in the presentation, and the church voting in a Sunday meeting.

The first step, led by a steering committee (with the counsel of a staff member), is what is called the KNOW-KNOW PHASE. The idea is to inspire all the members of the church to know all they need to know about all the people they need to know.

1. The "Know Your Family" Phase

In the local community and anywhere they can be found. I have found a wonderful response to my efforts to get reacquainted with relatives unknown about for years, as well as those seen with some regularity. The process has not been nearly completed, but it has been a joyful experience. It is not meddlesome, just an effort to make contact, show interest, and reestablish contact on a permanent basis. In the process you learn about their lives and needs.

Just recently we visited an uncle in a nursing home whom we had not seen in more than forty years. The eighty-nine-year-old man who has lived in a distant state for years assured us that he is a child of God. A few years back an eighty-seven-year-old aunt revealed that she would like to be baptized. She said she had been saved years ago, but had never been immersed and felt she ought to be. This was arranged to her delight and that of her immediate family.

There are other illustrations, and they are all very wonderful experiences. Whether loved ones live in your community their needs must be approached in love, diplomacy, respect, and sensitivity. I have not experienced one negative reaction.

Ministry can never be done condescendingly, patronizingly, or superficially. There are millions of family members, many living in the same house with church members, who can be included in the KNOW-KNOW PHASE.

2. Know Your Neighborhood Phase

A chairperson is selected in each community. The Lake Hills community is used as an illustration. In the development there are about a hundred homes, the first ones having been built less than twenty-five years ago. All Magnolia members in the community were to attend a meeting. Nine out of a possible thirteen homes were represented. Altogether they were able, in that meeting, to reconstruct a pretty fair profile of the Lake Hill residents. Certain people gathered other necessary information later. The emphasis was upon the KNOWING aspect of the program. Everybody agreed to try to KNOW everyone in the community. Several member families of Magnolia didn't know each other very well. It was agreed that everyone would try to get acquainted with everyone in the community over a period of months, but that it would be done in an informal manner.

Already, there is an annual Lake Hills picnic. There is a paid participation program of security in the community. So it is not too difficult to establish some sort of get-better-acquainted relationship. Certain people agreed to get certain pertinent information. Some, it was learned, had already begun some personal witnessing with neighbors. Those not in attendance in the initial meeting were informed and several of them have already begun to participate.

3. Know Your Workplace Phase

The church steering committee prepares a list of all businesses and industries in the geographical community of Magnolia church. There are four major manufacturing industries, three of them nationally or internationally known, and the other, though locally owned, does business nationally and some outside the country. All of these businesses had well-known Magnolia members in their ranks as well as in their management. Magnolia members representing different phases of labor and management participate in the initial meetings for separate industry. All Magnolia members are then invited to a meeting representing each industry and plans are devised to KNOW the people who work there to begin an informal ministry force. Always a low profile must be kept and always the message is knowing and helping wherever needed, rather than what they can do to help the church. Always it is learned that some evangelistic and other ministry is already being done. This program increases and intensifies it.

There are several smaller businesses like cable television, post offices, numerous banks, drug stores, laundry and cleaning establishments, service stations, groceries, clinics, legal and medical offices, garages, shops and others. Some of these businesses have Magnolia members and some of them don't. In all cases certain members, usually not involved in the usual organizational life of the church, are assigned by the appropriate committees to begin making contacts with the people who work in these businesses.

What do you do with people who are regular and active members of other churches? You work just as hard in making friends, discovering needs, and trying to meet needs. Your primary goal is the same: you are trying to minister to people. Some surprises may come as to evangelistic prospects. Some of them may be your own members, or in some cases members of other congregations. But your primary goal is never proselytizing.

4. Know Your School Place Phase

In the Magnolia community there are several elementary schools, one junior high school, and one senior high school. Most of these schools have teachers and staff people who are Magnolia members, and all of them have pupils there. Again, discretion, respect, diplomacy, and the law will be honored. As Christians we will be ministers, whether those ministered to ever become members of our congregations or not. Many of them should not, but some of them should and will. Students should be in all planning and steering committee meetings. They usually make the most effective marketplace ministers at school and elsewhere.

5. There are various work and school entities in the larger geographical community, like hospitals, colleges, as well as retail businesses, where Magnolia members work, study, and trade. They may also comprise a part of the marketplace for ministry.

6. There are professional and other groups where they are not in the same business, but have other affinity connections. They also offer marketplace opportunities.

The Sacred Workplace

The burning bush in the wilderness was the holy ground of Moses' call to service. Traditionally, God's work is what is done at the church place or for the church. At the beginning, however, "God's work" was the creation of the world. Over and over we see biblical expressions like "the earth is the Lord's," and so forth. Early on in human history there were "worship" places where God was considered present in some special way. However, all of us would agree that God's work was done at the Red Sea, wherever the manna appeared in the wilderness, at the feeding of the multitudes, the healing of the sick, in the Ethiopian's carriage, at the Philippian jail, at Collossae when Philemon received the letter from Paul about Onesimus.

Most of us who grew up in church heard about God calling people to "special service." That meant preaching or missionary work. Then we learned it could include "sacred music." Those growing up in church now understand it to include ministers of religious education, ministers of youth, children, and so forth. Along the way, somewhere we learned that God might call someone to teach in a church-related college, or even be the president of one. Then we seemed to understand when some said they had been "called" to practice medicine or teach school. So one would be called to a service career. We could even understand how God might call people to be farmers to feed the world.

Most Christians would agree that there is something "special" about being called to some service in the kingdom of God that is to be a lifelong calling, and precludes the possibility of having any other career or occupation. In some cases, biblically and historically, people are called to a special ministry for life and they can have some other career or job. Paul's word about God gifting some as apostles, prophets, evangelists, pastor and teachers, for equipping all the people of God for ministry, is clear. Those might or might not mean they were to be "full-time" or bi-vocational. God sometimes has called people for some special assignment that was not lifelong in scope.

Now what about the banker, lawyer, policeman, governor, mechanic, grocer, carpenter, factory worker, secretary, accountant, consultant, waitress, chef, janitor, plumber? On and on the list could go. We are not raising a question about comparative importance. Who can measure that? It is not a question of what is most important to God. We cannot always (if ever) answer that either. We are raising a question about what might be considered a work of God, what might be sacred, what might be considered ministry.

In a Kansas City church a revival preacher spoke about some of these things one night. The next evening a lady who heard the evangelist called her pastor to say that she had been happier at work that day than in years. "Today for the first time in ten years I went to work feeling that I am important, that my job is important, and that I am serving God when I do my job." You see, if you need an automobile in your service for God, or for your family's well-being, the people who work at the factory, transport the cars, sell the cars, and service the cars may be serving God. It is just as true in labor as in management and vice versa. This recognition might simplify work at the negotiation table. Years ago a shoe manufacturing company, now merged out of existence, had regular meetings of labor and management at the factory, with a local pastor attending. They were perhaps trying to move in the right direction.

Is the workplace any different if the management or the workers are Christians or atheists? Is your workplace any different because you are a Christian? In recent years prayer breakfasts have become popular in political and business places. We even sometimes talk about conversion experiences. That is wonderful and exciting. Have you participated in one where it spills over into the area of being the agents of reconciliation in the office or assembly line?[139] Is it possible for political decisions and appointments to be made because the job is a work of God and for God, rather than a political party or factional payoff? Some great gains have been made in civil rights, and more recently in international affairs where the motives were particularly spiritual. We thank God for the progress anyway, but pray for political leaders who feel called and committed to God to serve for His glory and the good of the world.

Very likely the church can be the church more completely when it comes to recognize that it can be the affirmation group, support group, and accountability group for a group of workers or professional people who are serving for the glory of God, as well as the Sunday School teachers who do their job on Sunday morning. Both groups are necessary. This is God's world on Thursday as well as Sunday. We all need the worship experience of the worship place on Sunday. We can work for God at the workplace on Monday. The home can be the refresher place for both. All these places provide opportunities for the people of God to help other people become the people of God. Whatever relationships may be enjoyed and whatever other ministries may be performed, evangelism involves telling the good news about salvation from sin and the new life in Christ.

Notes

1. Matthews, C. E. *Every Christian's Job* (Nashville: Broadman Press, 1954).
2. Conant, J. E. *Every Member Evangelism* (New York: Harper & Row, 1922), 2.
3. Leonard Sanderson.
4. Davis, William Hershey, *A Beginner's Grammar of the Greek New Testament* (Nashville: The Sunday School Board, 1923) Introduction by A. T. Robertson.
5. From *Baptist Hymnal* (Nashville, 1975, Convention Press).
6. From personal notes taken by Dr. Leonard Sanderson as Dr. Stott preached.
7. Ibid.
8. Leonard Sanderson.
9. From *Baptist Hymnal* (Nashville, 1975, Convention Press).
10. Leonard Sanderson.
11. Source uncertain.
12. Ron Johnson.
13. Ron Johnson.
14. Ron Johnson.
15. Schaller, Lyle E., *It's a Different World!* (Nashville: Abingdon Press, 1987) 21-31.
16. Surgener, James M., *Lost!* (Nashville: Broadman Press, 1988) 18-19.
17. The Unchurched American . . . 10 Years Later. A study by Princeton Religious Research Center. Followed up an initial study called, The Unchurched American.
18. Fish, Roy, "Trends Toward Universalism" A paper presented to the Evangelism Conference, Midwestern Theological Seminary.
19. Ron Johnson.
20. From personal notes of Dr. Leonard Sanderson.
21. Green, Michael, *Evangelism in the Early Church* (Grand Rapids: William B. Eerdmans, 1970) 49.
22. Hobbs, Herschel, *New Testament Evangelism* (Nashville: Convention Press, 1960) 3.
23. Dobbins, Gaines S., *Good News to Change Lives* (Nashville: Broadman Press, 1976) xvi, Introduction.
24. Ibid. 20.

25. Ibid. 22.

26. Stagg, Frank, *New Testament Theology* (Nashville: Broadman Press) 32.

27. Miles, Delos, *Introduction to Evangelism* (Nashville: Broadman Press) 47.

28. Ibid. Stagg, 32.

29. Barclay, William, *Turning to God* (Westminster Press: 1964) 31.

30. Mullins, E. Y., *The Christian Religion in its Doctrinal Expression* (Nashville: Broadman Press, 1917) 338.

31. Ibid. Green, 148.

32. Packer, J. I., *Evangelism and the Sovereignty of God* (Inter-varsity Press, n.d.) 33, 35.

33. Leonard Sanderson.

34. Ibid. Barclay, 48.

35. Ibid. Stagg, 119.

36. Strong, A. H., *Systematic Theology* (The Judson Press, 1909) 832, 833.

37. From personal notes of Leonard Sanderson.

38. Leonard Sanderson.

39. From personal notes of Leonard Sanderson.

40. Leonard Sanderson.

41. Leonard Sanderson.

42. Leonard Sanderson.

43. Bornkamm, Gunther *Early Christian Experience* (New York: Harper & Row, 1969) 14.

44. Ibid. Bornkamm, 14.

45. Source uncertain.

46. Jeremias, Joachim, *Jerusalem in the Time of Jesus* (Philadelphia: Fortress Press, 1969) 74.

47. Ibid, 74.

48. Ibid, 78.

49. Renan, Ernest, *The Life of Jesus* (New York: Carlton House, 1927) p. 81-85.

50. Ibid.

51. Ibid.

52. Ibid.

53. Ibid. Renan, 89.

54. Ibid. Renan, 140-145.

55. Ibid. Renan, 174.

56. Luke 8:3 seems to say that those who followed Jesus saw to the financial needs of the group.

57. Prince, Matthew, *Winning Through Caring* (Grand Rapids: Baker Book House 1981) 89.

58. Ibid. Prince, 89.

59. Ibid. Prince, 85.

60. Green, Michael, *Evangelism Now & Then* (Downers Grove, Ill.: Inter-Varsity Press, 1979) 16.

61. This term, "Overhearing the Gospel" is from a book by the same title by Fred Craddock.

62. Ibid. Green, 21.

63. Ibid. Green, 65-66.
64. Ron Johnson.
65. Ibid. Green, 109.
66. Ibid. Green, 55.
67. Newman, A. H., *A Manual of Church History* vol. 1 (American Baptist Publication Society, 1989) 147.
68. Green, Michael, *Evangelism in the Early Church* (Grand Rapids: Eerdmans, 1970) 172.
69. Newman, A. H., A Manual of Church History (American Baptist Publication Society, 1989) Vol. I, 147.
70. Latourette, 84.
71. Newman, 168.
72. Newman, 142.
73. Ibid. Latourette, 114.
74. Ibid. Latourette, n.p.n.
75. Newman, 305*ff.*
76. Latourette, 158.
77. Latourette, 185.
78. Ibid. Latourette, 192.
79. Latourette, 186*f.*
80. Newman, 211*f.*
81. Latourette, Kenneth Scott, *A History of the Expansion of Christianity,* (New York: Harper and Bros.) Vol. II, 1938, 144.
82. Latourette, Vol II, 117.
83. Source uncertain.
84. Scharpff, Paulus, *History of Evangelism,* WM. B. Eerdmans, 1964, 9.
85. McGlothin, W. J., *The Course of Christian History,* (New York: The Macmillan Company, 1936), 81.
86. Scharpff, 10.
87. Scharpff, 23.
88. Scharpff, 25.
89. Newman, Vol. II, 527.
90. Scharpff, 30.
91. Source uncertain.
92. Latourette, Vol. III, 82.
93. Latourette, Vol. III, 160.
94. Latourette, Vol. III, 168.
95. Latourette, Vol. III, 160*ff.*
96. Latourette, Vol. III, 167.
97. Latourette, Vol. III, 171.
98. Sweet, W. W., *Revivalism in America,* Charles Scribners and Sons, Preface.
99. Muncy, W. L., *A History of Evangelism in the United States,* (Kansas City; Central Seminary Press, 1945) 3.
100. Latourette, Vol. III, 207.
101. Latourette, Vol. III, 207.

102. Sweet, 14.

103. Muncy, *Chart in Introduction*.

104. Sweet, 14.

105. Sweet, 29.

106. Muncy, 28.

107. Leonard Sanderson.

108. Leavell, Roland Q., *Evangelism, Christ's Imperative Commission* (Nashville: Broadman Press, 1979) 84.

109. Ibid. Newman, n.p.n.

110. Ibid. Leavell, 84.

111. Ibid. Sweet, 127.

112. Ibid. Leavell, 96.

113. Leonard Sanderson.

114. Finney, Charles, 477.

115. Ibid. Pollack, 29.

116. Mann, 37*ff*.

117. Ibid. Mann, 50, or Pollack, 86.

118. Leonard Sanderson.

119. Leonard Sanderson.

120. As told by C. E. Matthews.

121. From Leonard Sanderson's notes.

122. Dale, Robert *To Dream Again* (Nashville: Broadman Press, 1981) 88.

123. Ron Johnson.

124. Ron Johnson.

125. Ron Johnson.

126. Edge, Findley, *The Doctrine of the Laity* (Nashville: Convention Press) 66.

127. Smith, Timothy, *Revivalism and Social Reform*, n.p.n.

128. Notes from a sermon preached by Charles Roesel.

129. Notes from an article printed in the *Florida Baptist Witness*.

130. From a paper that Nathan Porter gave to the Home Mission Board staff.

131. Ibid.

132. Ron Johnson.

133. Dale, Robert and Delos Miles, *Evangelizing the Hard to Reach* (Nashville: Broadman Press, 1986) 127-128.

134. Ibid.

135. From a song by Cynthia Clawson.

136. Edge, Findley B. *The Greening of the Church* (Word, 1971); *The Doctrine of the Laity* (Broadman Press, 1985).

137. Garland, David E., *Review and Expositor*, (Fall, 1974) 523.

138. Carver, W. O., *The Glory of God in the Christian Calling* (Broadman Press, 1949) 148.

139. Bernbaum and Steer, *Why Work?* (Grand Rapids: Baker Book House, 1986) 60.

Index of Names and Places

A

Abraham 65*ff.*
Adams, J. McKee 67
Alger, Horatio 72
Ambrose of Milan 105,107
Anabaptists 115-116
Antioch of Pisidia 89
Apostles 85
Appelman, Hyman 147
Appleseed, Johnny 89
Apostles 85
Arabs 81
Athenasius 107
Augustine, Bishop of Hippo 105,107
Augustus, Caesar, Emperor of Rome 76-77
Aurelius, Marcus, Emperor of Rome 98
Autrey, C. E. 150

B

Baptist, John the (or John the Baptizer) 82-83
Baptists, American 131-132
Barnabas (or Joseph, "The Encourager") 90,91
Beecher, Lyman 133
Bernard of Clairvaux 110
Bethlehem 81
Bishop of Constantinople 105
Blair, John 128
Blair, Samuel 128
Bohemian Brethren 116
Broughton, Len 143
Bryan, O. E. 144,145

C

Caesarea 94

Calvin, John 115,116
Carey, William 131
Carver, W. O. 184
Celsus 103
Chafin, Kenneth 150-151
Christian Movement 99
Chrysostom, John 105,107
Clarke, John 130
Clement of Alexandria 107
Clement of Rome 107
Coble, William 61
Coddington, William 124
Conant, J. E. 15
Congress on Evangelism 24
Constantine, Emperor of Rome 103-104
Constantinople, Bishop of 105
Cornelius 94
Crenshaw, William 123
Cyril of Alexandria 107

D

Dale, Robert 156
Dargan, E. C. 144
Davies, Samuel 128
De Labadie, Jean 117-118
De La Warr ???
Dickinson, Jonathan
Diocletian, Emperor of Rome ?
Dionysius of Alexandria 107
Disciples Movement 133
Dobbins, Gaines S. 42
Dodd, M. E. 146
Dominicus of Spain 110
Donatists 112
Dossey, E. Y. 149

E

Eastman, Fred 146

Index of Subjects